The Language of Sport

This accessible satellite textbook in the Routledge INTERTEXT series is unique in offering students hands-on practical experience of textual analysis focused on the language of sport. Written in a clear, user-friendly style by a practising teacher and examiner, it combines practical activities with texts, accompanied by commentaries and suggestions for research. It can be used individually or in conjunction with the series core textbook, *Working with Texts: A core book for language analysis*.

Aimed at A-Level and beginning undergraduate students, *The Language of Sport*:

◎   looks at sport in its wider social context
◎   examines the way sport sells itself as an agent of social cohesion and is used to sell products
◎   explores how sporting texts construct ideas about gender and national identity
◎   uses examples from events as diverse as Wimbledon tennis, Euro 96 and the World Athletics Championships
◎   has a comprehensive glossary of terms

Adrian Beard is Head of English at Gosforth High School in Newcastle-upon-Tyne. He is Principal Moderator at the Northern Examining and Assessment Board for A-Level English Literature Coursework.

The Intertext series

◎ **Why does the phrase 'spinning a yarn' refer both to using language and making cloth?**

◎ **What might a piece of literary writing have in common with an advert or a note from the milkman?**

◎ **What aspects of language are important to understand when analysing texts?**

The Routledge INTERTEXT series will develop readers' understanding of how texts work. It does this by showing some of the designs and patterns in the language from which they are made, by placing texts within the contexts in which they occur, and by exploring relationships between them.

The series consists of a foundation text, *Working with Texts: A core book for language analysis*, which looks at language aspects essential for the analysis of texts, and a range of satellite texts. These apply aspects of language to a particular topic area in more detail. They complement the core text and can also be used alone, providing the user has the foundation skills furnished by the core text.

Benefits of using this series:

◎ **Unique** – written by a team of respected teachers and practitioners whose ideas and activities have also been trialled independently

◎ **Multi-disciplinary** – provides a foundation for the analysis of texts, supporting students who want to achieve a detailed focus on language

◎ **Accessible** – no previous knowledge of language analysis is assumed, just an interest in language use

◎ **Comprehensive** – wide coverage of different genres: literary texts, notes, memos, signs, advertisements, leaflets, speeches, conversation

◎ **Student-friendly** – contains suggestions for further reading; activities relating to texts studied; commentaries after activities; key terms highlighted and an index of terms

The series editors:

Ronald Carter is Professor of Modern English Language in the Department of English Studies at the University of Nottingham and is the editor of the Routledge INTERFACE series in Language and Literary Studies. He is also co-author of *The Routledge History of Literature in English*. From 1989 to 1992 he was seconded as National Director for the Language in the National Curriculum (LINC) project, directing a £21.4 million in-service teacher education programme.

Angela Goddard is Senior Lecturer in Language at the Centre for Human Communication, Manchester Metropolitan University, and was Chief Moderator for the project element of English Language A-Level for the Northern Examination and Assessment Board (NEAB) from 1983 to 1995. Her publications include *The Language Awareness Project: Language and Gender*, vols I and II, 1988, and *Researching Language*, 1993 (Framework Press).

First series title:

Working with Texts: A core book for language analysis
Ronald Carter, Angela Goddard, Danuta Reah, Keith Sanger, Maggie Bowring

Satellite titles:

The Language of Sport
Adrian Beard

The Language of Newspapers
Danuta Reah

The Language of Advertising: Written texts
Angela Goddard

The Language of Humour
Alison Ross

The Language of Poetry
John McRae

The Language of Fiction
Keith Sanger

Related titles:

INTERFACE series:

Variety in Written English
Tony Bex

Literary Studies in Action
Alan Durant and Nigel Fabb

Language, Literature and Critical Practice
David Birch

English in Speech and Writing
Rebecca Hughes

A Linguistic History of English Poetry
Richard Bradford

Feminist Stylistics
Sara Mills

The Language of Jokes
Delia Chiaro

Language in Popular Fiction
Walter Nash

The Discourse of Advertising
Guy Cook

Textual Intervention
Rob Pope

Literature about Language
Valerie Shepherd

The Language of Sport

● Adrian Beard

LONDON AND NEW YORK

First published 1998
by Routledge
11 New Fetter Lane, London EC4P 4EE

Simultaneously published in the USA and
Canada
by Routledge
29 West 35th Street, New York, NY 10001

© 1998 Adrian Beard

Typeset in Stone Sans/Stone Serif by
Solidus (Bristol) Limited

Printed and bound in Great Britain by
TJ International Ltd., Padstow, Cornwall

*British Library Cataloguing in Publication
Data*

A catalogue record for this book is
available from the British Library

*Library of Congress Cataloguing in Publication
Data*

Beard, Adrian, 1951–
    The language of sport/Adrian Beard.
        p.   cm. – (Intertext)

    Includes bibliographical references
and index.

    1.   English language – Discourse
analysis.   2.   Sports – Terminology.
3.   Sports – Language.
    I.   Title.   II.   Series: Intertext (London,
England)
PE1422.B43   1998
401'. 41 – dc21
                                        97-15837
                                             CIP

ISBN 0–415–16911–9

contents

Unit seven: Sportswriting I   83

Unit eight: Sportswriting II   99

acknowledgements

Particular thanks to Angela Goddard for her help at all stages in the writing of this book and to Ronald Carter for his useful suggestions.

Grateful thanks to all the English Language A-Level students of Gosforth High School who have contributed data to this book, especially Kerry Balfour, David Blight, Emily Bruce, Richard Elvin and Neil Heckels.

The author and publishers wish to thank the following for permission to reprint copyright material:

Nike UK for 'Understand Now'; Fila UK Ltd. for 'The best F in shoes'; Compaq for 'A Program for Every Fan'; Guinness Brewing Great Britain for 'Wesley Widget'; the *Independent* for 'The Leading Lady of British Hockey' by Simon O'Hagan; Rex Features for 'Stu or Die' by John Askill in the *Sun*; the *Independent* for 'A Very English Hero' by Robert Winder; Mark Steel for 'Fred's A Right Sri Lanka' in *JM96** no. 44 (November 1995); Euro 96 Commentary T1 and Radio Commentary Courtesy of the BBC, with thanks to Barry Davies and Trevor Brooking, Mike Ingham and Steve Coppell; ITV Network Sport for Euro 96 Commentary T2; Egmont Fleetway Ltd for 'Roy of the Rovers' (c); Victor Gollancz Ltd and Nick Hornby for *Fever Pitch*; Belleville News-Democrat for 'Baseball Report'; Mainstream Publishing Co. Ltd for *Dark Trade* by Donald McRae; Reed Consumer Books and Pete Davies for *I Lost My Heart To The Belles*.

This sporting life

Sport is usually on the back page of our newspapers, away from all the serious stuff like war, politics and scandal. It is placed in a world of its own. And people involved in sport often like to claim that it is outside the web of issues which make up our culture. 'Keep politics out of sport' was a common cry from those who wished to play sport against South Africa in the years of apartheid, for instance, and when violence occurs on the field of play, sports administrators do all they can to ensure that the perpetrators are not dealt with by the police and the legal system.

Sport is often associated with words like 'recreation', 'leisure', 'play'. One dictionary defines it as 'a game, merry-making, a frolic', in other words an activity or activities that are about fun, light-heartedness, escape from reality. Sometimes sport does indeed offer physical relaxation and a sense of escape from the pressures of the real world, but all sport, and especially serious competitive sport, is tied in with the complex systems of human behaviour that we call 'society'.

Any full analysis of sport's place in society today would need to recognise a huge network of factors. The most important concern economics and money, including the advertising and selling of merchandise, the wages of players, the way sport has been used by satellite television stations and much more. Other factors include sport's role in establishing regional and national identity; the historical development of sport; the way the media cover sport; issues of gender, race, age and class; politics and power in sport; sport's place in our education system.

This book looks in particular at the language surrounding sport, but language does not exist in a vacuum - it reflects society. Language is the means by which many of the factors outlined in the previous paragraph are established, negotiated and maintained. This book will explore some of these factors within a sporting context. But remember, as you work with the different units, that there are underlying features which could just as well be applied to many other fields of human activity. Sport, despite its place on the back page, does not really exist in a world of its own.

This unit will look at some of the ways in which society constructs a set of values around sport and at some of the ways sport is used to promote commercial products.

It's not cricket

The terms **denotation** and **connotation** will be used frequently in this section. Denotation and connotation are terms which relate to the study of meaning or **semantics**. Denotation is the referential meaning, the barest core of a word's meaning. Connotation refers to the level of meaning based on associations we attach to words.

The word 'cricket' is of uncertain origin . The most likely origin is from the French game 'criquet', but others claim that the word is from the Saxon word 'cricc', a shepherd's crook, perhaps because the game is so often associated, in the UK, with England and Englishness.

So, a denotation of the game 'cricket' could be 'a game played between two teams of eleven players'. Connotations associated with the game, however, are likely to produce very different responses.

Activity

Working in groups or pairs, if possible, brainstorm the connotations that arise from the word 'cricket'. Write the word in the centre of a sheet of paper, and write in spidergram form the various ideas that are suggested.

Commentary

When sixth-form students in a Newcastle school were asked to brainstorm the connotations that arise when they think of the game of cricket, the following appeared most frequently in their lists.

Lord's   tradition   upper class   village green   middle-aged men

cream teas   civilised   public schools   ladies in hats   John Major

Whites   conservatism   CRICKET   it's not cricket   England

middle-class   formal   etiquette   southern England   scones

on a sticky wicket   classical game   Yorkshire *v.* Lancashire

The most frequent connotations the students had for cricket are that it is played by men, of a high/middle-class status, on village greens, in rural southern England. They also associated the game with good sportsmanship and social etiquette, as shown in some of the **metaphors** of cricket (such as 'it's not cricket') which are in common use outside a sporting context.

The students' findings can be grouped under various headings. 'Upper class', 'public schools' (and possibly 'civilised', 'sportsmanship', 'etiquette' and even 'scones and cream teas') relate to social class; 'countryside', 'southern England', 'village green', 'Lord's', 'Yorkshire *v.* Lancashire' relate to region and location; 'men', 'middle-aged men' and 'old ladies in hats' relate to age and gender. References to 'tradition', 'conservatism' and 'John Major' are to do with politics.

These groupings reinforce the idea that sport is shaped by social and political influences but the real picture of cricket as a modern sport is rather different from the connotations the students had. It is particularly strong in industrial areas such as the north of England, as well as in Wales and Scotland. Black and Asian players have made a huge impact on the British professional and amateur game. The major grounds are all in big cities. Many women play the game. Clearly an image of the game has developed which does not give a full and accurate picture of its place in society.

Why is this? National, or sometimes regional myths help to create a sense of shared purpose and group identity. This identity is also useful in selling a game or an event. Advertisers of a product like to establish what is sometimes called a unique selling proposition, a quick and often simple sense of what a product will mean to prospective purchasers. This can range from slogans and catch-phrases to a more sophisticated image where the product is at the centre of a whole way of life. Sport, like any other product, must be sold by projecting a certain view of itself. Potential 'buyers' will include sponsors, television companies and spectators.

In its early days cricket was renowned for betting, cheating and crowd trouble, yet by the beginning of this century 'It's not cricket' was a

3

phrase in common use to suggest anti-social behaviour. The view of the game shown by the Newcastle students is particularly strong in literature. Cricket matches in novels — and there are many examples — are nearly always examples of ideal rural life; Siegfried Sassoon, A.G. Macdonell and L.P. Hartley have all written in this vein.

Books which take this view are still being written. A recently published (1995) novel called *The Village Cricket Tour* by Vernon Coleman was reviewed as 'a whimsical novel which describes the adventures and mishaps of a village cricket team who spend two weeks of their summer holidays on a cricket tour of the most picturesque spots in the west country'. Even the normally gloomy playwright Harold Pinter strikes a more idyllic tone when writing about cricket.

This idealised view of cricket is sustained in a number of ways, despite the huge changes the game has undergone in recent years. Television and radio commentators tend to project an image of the game based on a narrow view of its social position. For many years a standard phrase, before an update of events, was 'For those of you who have just come in from the office . . .', as though only senior civil servants watched the game. Even the replacement phrase 'For those of you who have just come in from work . . .' makes assumptions about employment. Prime Minister John Major in the 1990s evoked an image of 'cricketers' shadows lengthening over a village green' as part of his definition of the best of English life. The women's game, meanwhile, is rarely reported.

The idealised view of cricket serves both the game and the media which report it. It is much easier to sell the game, and to commentate on it, when it has a unique selling proposition. Even when the media home in on a scandal, and there have been several in cricket in recent years, they reinforce the stereotype by stressing that scandalous behaviour deviates from normal behaviour. Much has been written recently about tampering with the ball in cricket and so allowing bowlers an unfair advantage — 'it's not cricket'. Although many players admit to bending the rules, the media have presented the issue as a few dishonest players ruining the game's good name. Pakistan players have often been singled out for particular criticism in Britain, with some coverage verging on the racist. Coverage of the same stories in Pakistan, of course, portrays them in a very different light.

Our connotations about cricket, then, involve a whole set of values that have come from, among other things, its economic and historical development, from the way the media cover it, from what politicians say, from what we read in literature, and from the image that the sport itself wishes to encourage.

You will find below the names of some popular sports. For each one, write down any connotations, such as the ones noted about cricket, that form instantly in your mind when you think of the sport. These might include aspects such as the typical age of the players/watchers, places where the sport is most played, the social class of the players/watchers, the gender of the players/watchers and any others.

> greyhound racing; snooker; golf; netball; rugby league; rugby union; skiing; basketball; polo; crown green bowls; hockey; fishing; Wimbledon tennis; motor racing; baseball

Compare your answers with others in your group. What patterns of connotation emerge? Where there are fields of meaning, such as class, gender, age, regional identity, etc., group them together to produce a picture of the sport's typical image.

Collect as many newspaper reports as you can which cover your chosen sport. (For the less popular ones you may need to look at specialist magazines.) See how many of the connotations you listed are clearly endorsed by the language of the articles, and how many are endorsed in a more subtle way, by implication, for instance. If the sport has 'alternative' coverage, such as fanzines, see if they in any way challenge the expected view of the sport.

Fields of dreams

Many other sports are similar to cricket in the way they have developed a traditional image. A number of football clubs in major industrial cities, for instance, have had a traditional image associated with mass working-class support standing on open terraces. A combination of events forced changes, though. Safety measures required by law after the Heysel and Hillsborough disasters in the 1980s, satellite television's financial input, the takeover of some clubs by millionaire entrepreneurs, have led to all-seater stadiums, expensive season tickets, corporate marketing.

All these factors are altering the traditional base of support, and the power structure which runs the game. Newcastle United Football Club, for instance, was a typical northern club with large working-class support. Now, however, the only way to see a match is to buy a season ticket, which means that those on low or no income cannot afford to attend matches. Nonetheless much of the language surrounding the reporting of their games still dwells on the old image of working-class support, fanatical fans, regional identity. Sir John Hall, the club's millionaire owner, often reinforces this paradox between commercial expansion and traditional roots; in a radio interview he said the club's success is 'bringing tremendous pride for the region, tremendous publicity for the region and will help to develop the region economically, culturally and develop the pride of the Geordie nation'.

The region he refers to, the north-east of England is one of Britain's most socially deprived areas. In referring to the 'Geordie nation', Sir John Hall is suggesting that there is a regional unity and pride which his football club helps to reinforce (see Unit 3 for a further discussion of this topic). It is unlikely that sporting success, and subsequent regional patriotism, do anything to alleviate the social poverty of the area, however. Modern sport, with its increasing financial involvement, is part of an economic and commercial system which accepts social deprivation as a necessary evil. Sport endorses the social status quo rather than challenging or reshaping it.

The **rhetoric** of sport and those involved in it, though, often tries to present a view of sport as an agent of social change. In the same radio interview Sir John Hall said 'Sport is a field which in a sense we can offer kids, because if you don't offer kids anything they'll continue to steal your cars, break into your house and continue to feel neglected. We can help to fulfil some of their dreams'. The kids to whom he refers are unlikely to attend games or become players – their only contact with their team is likely to be through watching commercial television stations whose advertising offers them a material world outside their reach. Big-business football teams have few links with deprived inner city areas these days. Dreams, by their very nature, are not fulfilled.

One of the ironic consequences of this is that identity with the club is far more likely to come from wearing its merchandise than from going to games. This suits the clubs well; they profit not only from the season-ticket sales but also from the sales of an ever increasing, ever changing range of clothing. The Football Association announced at the end of 1996 that it intended to change the national team strip early in 1997. Because England had reached the semi-finals of Euro 96, a large number of team strips were sold, especially near Christmas. Many young fans were therefore given presents costing £70 which would be outdated a month later.

Professionalism in Rugby Union has led to similar tensions between clubs, governing bodies and supporters. A sport whose image was linked to amateurism and the middle classes now has to face the economic realities of professional sport and already various factions are fighting for control of the game. As has already been seen in cricket and football, control of a professional sport is very closely tied to television rights – in other words it is the money which television provides which is the real driving force behind the sport's development. So any academic analysis of sport, including the language of sport, must take into account the fact that sports, whatever connotations may surround them, are not in a world of their own, but are part of the social, economic and cultural systems which shape our lives.

Advertising and sport

Advertising is one obvious field where social, economic and cultural systems can be seen to interlock. Sport is big business and many companies use sport as a means of publicising their product. Sports teams are sponsored by firms, and wear the product's name on their shirts. A large number of tournaments and events are sponsored by companies, with tobacco companies particularly prominent; because they are not allowed to advertise on television, tobacco companies use sporting events to promote cigarettes. Many leagues and organisations carry a sponsor's name, with alcoholic drinks particularly prominent.

A typical sports magazine, such as the football magazine *Four Four Two*, carries adverts which fall broadly into two categories: adverts which promote sports equipment, especially footwear, and adverts which use sport as a basis to advertise more general commodities. What all the adverts have in common, though, is that they are aimed at the magazine's typical reader; in this case a relatively affluent, male, adult football follower. The adverts which are looked at in this unit are all taken from editions of *Four Four Two*.

The sports firm Nike have a considerable share of the sportswear market. Nike, incidentally, was the Greek goddess of victory. The following advert is one of a series whereby the dreams of a young boy are placed alongside the success of a star player. In this instance the player is David Ginola, a Frenchman who was playing for Newcastle United. The written text, printed here, formed the right-hand margin of a double-page advert showing a young boy looking in a mirror and seeing reflected back at him the face of Ginola. Ginola had a reputation for classical good looks and had been a model as well as a footballer.

Text: Nike

UNDERSTAND THIS NOW. WHEN YOU CROSS THE BALL, IT'LL BE 'LOOK, DAVID GINOLA'S BOOTS'. NOT 'LOOK, DAVID GINOLA'.

There are people who dream of playing like Ginola. But won't.

There are people who think they can already play like Ginola. But can't.

There are people, on a pitch somewhere, alone, right now, who are trying hard to play like Ginola.

And might.

Skill doesn't come from dreaming or just putting your feet into the right boots. It comes from practice and putting your heart into something you believe in.

When David Ginola was seven, he told his best friend he was going to make it. Twelve gruelling, painful, bloody, sweaty years later, his friend believed him.

So. You want to cross the ball like Ginola? Go out and cross the ball. A thousand times. Then a thousand times the next day. And the next.

You want to score goals like Ginola? Like his volley against Madrid? Find goalposts and hurt them.

You want speed and stamina? Then run.

And while you're running, ask yourself this. Are you ready for boots like Ginola?

Nike Air Rio. Soft leather. Wide last. Air cushioned.

Fit O.K.? Good.

Another thousand crosses please.

Just do it.

1   What details are given about the manufacturers of the boots and about the boots themselves?
2   How does the advert use David Ginola as part of its advertising technique?
3   The advert constructs a reader in its use of 'you'. What can you work out about this constructed reader and how does the advert contain a series of commands given to this constructed reader?

Little is actually said about the boots themselves, and the makers' name is only mentioned once in the text, and even then not prominently. The boots are called Nike Air Rio, have 'soft leather', 'a wide last' and are 'air cushioned'. The advert is not selling a technical specification, as much as an image, an image that has been reinforced through many other adverts in print and on television. The company are confident that readers will recognise their logo (a red tick) and their slogan ('Just do it') and know the brand name without having to place any great emphasis on it.

The idea of the star performer endorsing equipment is an old one – 'as used by'. David Ginola is referred to in more subtle ways here, though. The headline makes it clear that the aspiring young footballer will never look exactly like Ginola, either as handsome model or as star player, while the following text offers only the possibility of playing 'like' him. Dreamers 'won't' play like him, the arrogant 'can't' play like him, those working hard just 'might'. At best, though, it will be the boots, the object of the advert, which will give any real likeness. Because the advert is emphasising the need for practice, it makes it clear that although Ginola's looks are natural, his ability has come through hard work. It tells a brief 'story' of how Ginola made it because of the 'gruelling, painful, bloody, sweaty' years of practice that he was prepared to put in. These words all belong to the same **semantic field**, one of toil and lack of glamour. Ginola, then, is presented as a unique player, who has skill and dedication but whose career offers a moral message – skill 'doesn't come from dreaming', but from 'putting your heart into something you believe in'. 'Putting your feet into the right boots' is not enough; if you want to be in Ginola's shoes you must work and struggle.

Many written adverts contain linguistic features similar to spoken language. In this advert, for instance, the **imperative** voice is clearly meant to imitate someone shouting a set of orders. In the advert for

Compaq computers which follows later in this unit the first words 'So computers aren't your thing' also have the sense of being spoken. Most students will be familiar, possibly through studying literature, with the idea that the voice who 'speaks' a text is not necessarily the author. The invented speaker of the text is often called the **narrator** or the **narrative persona**. But just as a constructed voice can deliver the text, so a constructed reader can receive it. This constructed reader, a constructed figure who can often be placed in terms of age, gender, class, values, can be referred to as as the **narratee**.

Although this is an advert aimed at the readers of an adult magazine, the text constructs a narratee who is much younger. The advert's main text moves from a number of references to 'There are people', through a brief story about Ginola's past, before coming to address the narratee, who appears to be a young boy wanting to be a professional footballer. The large photograph which was printed alongside the text endorsed this view. The imperative voice of command is used to dispel dreams, it is the harsh voice of reality, an instructor of the old school who demands at the beginning that the narratee should 'Understand Now', and states at the end that he should 'Just do it'. There are also many more commands which follow rhetorical questions, such as 'Go out and cross the ball', 'Find goalposts and hurt them', 'Then run'. Only when you are 'fit', in the sense of both physical fitness and suitability are you then ready to see if the boots fit. And then you return to practice, as qualifying to wear the boots is the start of yet more hard work.

This imperative effect, a young boy being given no-nonsense realism, is helped by the way a number of paragraphs end with short **elliptical** statements: 'But won't', 'But can't' and the verb phrase 'And might' acting as a paragraph on its own. As the text reaches a conclusion, paragraphs and 'sentences' become shorter. The description of the boot, for instance, has four **noun phrases**, each followed by a full stop; this too gives a sense of hard facts, of the Nike boot being a necessary part of the attempt to be a star.

As a whole, then, the advert does not really address young boys but it creates, with great skill, a fiction which will appeal to older and more affluent readers. The fiction's world is peopled by imagined readers, imagined instructors and a real player, although even he has a fictionalised story told about him. Although at first glance this may appear to be a straightforward piece of advertising, it is in fact a very sophisticated text.

The advert for Fila footwear which follows was also published in *Four Four Two*. It was originally in colour.

Activity

Make some brief notes about the language used in this advert. Look in particular at its design and ways in which it is aimed at its likely audience.

Commentary

Unlike the Nike advert, where the product's name appeared only once, the product name features a number of times in this advert. It is shown three times on the shoe itself, and is displayed again at the bottom of the advert. The letter F is highlighted in two ways. When in colour the top stroke of the letter is red, whereas the rest of the letter and other letters are in black. Also the company logo at the bottom of the advert contains a large F on its own as well as the complete word Fila. This means that the main identification mark for Fila shoes is the letter F.

The main text of the advert takes the letter F, already identified as important, and places it at the centre of the eye-catching statement 'the best F in shoes . . .' The letter F is actually placed in the middle line of the statement, and 'in' is added alongside. All of the letters are in **lower case** except for F which again gives it more prominence. The actual words form a phrase rather than a clause – there is no verb – and the sense that this is part of a larger statement is given by the lower case at the beginning and the row of dots at the end. This suggests that there is more to say about these shoes, but this is the main point.

There are a number of meanings that can be taken from 'the best F in shoes . . .', a phrase which has been constructed with deliberate ambiguity. The row of dots after the word 'shoes' could suggest the reader's thought process as various possibilities are weighed up. One involves the use of F as an identification of the brand, suggesting that there may be other companies with F in their name, but Fila are the best. On a literal level the word 'shoes' does not contain the letter F, which again makes the reader think. The most obvious meaning, though, involves hearing the sound of the statement. When people wish to give the impression of swearing, but in fact fall short of saying the whole word, they use the form 'f–––ing'. Many regional accents would omit the last letter, which would make 'f–––in'. So in fact Fila are the best fucking shoes, although cleverly they have not said as such; it is the reader who must supply the full word. Given that the magazine is aimed at young adult males it is likely that the readers will do so without offence. The statement is so effective because in a very few words it creates both impact and ambiguity, making the reader reflect, if only for the split second that it takes to process the language, before moving on to the next page.

There is also a deliberate ambiguity surrounding the slogan 'change the game'. Many sportsgoods manufacturers have slogans, and the fact that they are often in the form of an imperative makes them dynamic and purposeful. Because there is no agent identified here, just who or what is changing the game is left ambiguous – is it you the purchaser, the Fila shoe, or a combination of both? And how do you change the game? Are you changing the rules, playing another game altogether, or winning rather than losing?

The adverts for Nike and Fila are about sports shoes, but many companies use sport to promote other commodities. The following advert for Compaq computers appeared in *Four Four Two* in early 1996. Technically this advert is known as an **advertorial**, because it was prepared and written by the magazine's staff rather than by an agency operating on behalf of the company. Alongside this page of text was a full page picture of a Queens Park Rangers footballer; at the time of this advert the team was sponsored by Compaq.

Activity

If possible, discuss the following questions in groups and then compare your findings with other groups.

1 How does the advert construct the idea of a typical reader – or narratee? What can you detect about the narratee's constructed identity, such as age, gender, social class, degree of affluence, interests?

2 How does the advert use the language of football to maintain the link between the computer and the football magazine reader, and how does it use the technical language of computing?

3 How does this advert create a sense of being a spoken text, rather than a written one?

4 The American linguist Deborah Tannen says in her book *You Just Don't Understand* that her research has shown her that many men look at the world in a hierarchical way in which they are either 'one-up or one-down'. Male conversations, she says, are often 'negotiations in which people try to achieve and maintain the upper hand if they can', whereas female conversations are 'negotiations for closeness in which women try to give confirmation and support'. Where in this advert can you find examples of language that is to do with outdoing others?

13

A PROGRAM FOR EVERY FAN

SO COMPUTERS aren't your thing – you'd never use one, you're not interested, they're simply not for you. Maybe. But then again computers have changed a little since you last played Pac-man or Asteroids on your school mate's ZX81!

The latest multimedia computers are a breed apart from the computers of the past – so here's a fresh look at what a computer could do for you.

Compaq is top of the league when it comes to multimedia and, like the best teams in the Premiership, its Presario range of home computers combines entertainment with excellence. Each Compaq Presario comes with an inbuilt modem allowing access to CompuServe, the Internet and e-mail. It also includes a hands free telephone, an answering machine and fax so you can arrange where to meet your mates before the match. The Spatializer 3-D Stereo Surround Sound will give all your music CDs an extra edge and completely immerse you in multimedia games and CD-ROMs.

And there's something for everyone, whether you want to impress your girlfriend by cooking a great meal (coached from the screen by a top chef) or choosing a good wine (with the help of Oz Clarke). You can even re-live your favourite movie moments or look up the latest Hollywood releases on the World Wide Web. The Compaq Presario boasts MPEG which allows you to experience the best full motion video action.

But, if football's your one and only love don't panic – there are some great footy games to play solo or against your mates. You can guide your favourite team to cup or league glory or even try to outwit Terry Venables and prove your theories on where the England team is going wrong – just what you need to help you overcome the traditional close season withdrawal symptoms.

The Compaq Presario comes with word processing, database and spreadsheet software and also includes a French and German language CD-ROM which could help with those European fixtures or to translate exactly what the Premiership's latest foreign imports are saying to the ref. Financial software helps you to plan your accounts – to see if the next away match is within your grasp. And Encarta – the Encyclopaedia CD-ROM – will help you impress your mates on the terraces with your general knowledge gems at half-time. You can even watch a video clip of Maradona's "hand of God" goal and ponder life's injustices.

The Compaq Presario comes with a Pentium processor meaning it has the speed to cope with the most powerful programs and games.

To find more about the Compaq Presario range of multimedia home computers visit any leading high street electrical retailer.

COMPAQ

14

5   Looking at your research on all the above questions, how has this advert been constructed to sell to a specific audience?

The final advert in this unit is for Guinness Bitter. It is one of a series depicting the exploits of Wesley Widget and should be read in conjunction with the Roy of the Rovers extract in Unit 7 on writing about sport (Text, pp. 88–89). **Intertextuality** involves reading one text through knowledge of another and the Wesley Widget series has used the reader's knowledge of comic strip conventions to create a deliberately humorous effect. There is a considerable amount of linguistic play in this advert, especially using language from two different semantic fields at the same time. When the penalty 'didn't even touch the sides', for instance, there is a reference to the ball entering the goal and to the expression for drinking beer quickly. There are many **puns** – bitter've/bit of a – and also references to other Guinness advertising campaigns in the use of the word 'genius'.

Activity

Prepare notes on the following questions:

1   List the various puns and double meanings that can be found in this advert.
2   What do you notice about the proper nouns (the names of people, places) that are used?
3   How does the advert use some of the conventions of the comic strip to create humour?

Now write a commentary on the advert using your notes as a basis for your answer.

Extension

Advertising offers the opportunity to collect lots of data related to sport. Some, like the adverts for Nike and Fila, advertise sports equipment, others, like the Compaq and Guinness adverts, use sport to advertise other goods.

In a language project you could look at the way language is used to promote sports and their equipment, or the way sport is used to sell items which are not in themselves sporting. In both cases, you will be looking at the way language contributes to the associations which surround various sports and their players.

Sporting figures

Linguistic research conducted in the past thirty or so years has shown how gender affects language use in a whole range of formal and informal contexts. The central tenet of this book is that sport does not exist in a world of its own but reflects the world around it. If there are gender issues in our society, then these issues are likely to appear in sport; and if language is central to human behaviour, then the language of sport is likely to provide interesting evidence for how we view men and women differently.

Research projects and investigations on sporting topics are popular with English-language students, with issues surrounding gender being particularly popular. When these are well focused and rooted in clearly organised data they can be very helpful in showing how sport reflects the wider world around it.

One of the first problems faced by students who wish to research the way men and women are represented in sport is that there is relatively little coverage of women in sport, and there are relatively few women who are sports journalists or commentators. Even at major events such as the Wimbledon Tennis Championships, women's events are usually commentated upon by men, with the role of summariser/expert sometimes taken by a female former player.

Activity

Over the period of one week, research how much coverage there is for men's and women's sport in a selection of media. You could include a tabloid newspaper, a broadsheet newspaper, BBC, Sky sports, etc. You will not need to watch all the events, as the listings will give you sufficient information in many cases.

At the same time see if you can collect some data on how many women are producers of sports material, in the sense of being journalists or main commentators. Look in particular at how many women write or commentate about women's events.

Anyone for tennis?

There are some sporting events which include competitions for both men and women, and these can be particularly useful for research purposes. Two of the most obvious to look at, because men and women compete at the same venue, are Wimbledon Tennis and a major athletics championship, and they will form the basis for most of the data in this unit.

With so much potential data – the coverage of sport is a major part of media output – it is important to focus on specific linguistic details when investigating the language of sport and gender. One linguistic system which is a useful starting point for the analysis of gender in sport is that of naming.

Names and naming systems are highly significant in our social interaction. Names, especially when used as terms of address, are markers of social power and relationships. A school or college, for instance, will have many naming conventions, which, when analysed, say a great deal about the relative status and power of both the named and the namer.

The following are some of the possible terms of address you would find in a school; alongside each are an example and an abbreviation so that they can be referred to more easily.

Title and last name	(TLN)	Miss Jones
Title first and last name	(TFLN)	Miss Rebecca Jones
Last name	(LN)	Roberts
First name	(FN)	Brian
First name and last name	(FNLN)	Brian Roberts
Title	(T)	Sir/Miss
Nickname	(NN)	Robbo
Endearment	(E)	Sweetie
Role	(R)	Headteacher

A teacher can use a student's first name, but a student, in a school at least, normally has to address a teacher via either a formal title and surname – 'Mr Smith' – or simply the title, 'Sir'. A teacher may have a nickname, but it is unlikely that the student will use it to their face. Teachers on the other hand may address students by nicknames, providing the student is comfortable with the name. These non-reciprocal exchanges, where people use different types of term of address, mark the fact that those involved do not have equal power and status. The various patterns of non-reciprocal use can be represented in diagrams, such as the one below, which is based on data collected by a sixth-form student in a Newcastle comprehensive school:

TLN   Headteacher   (The headteacher called members of
                                  the teaching staff by FN, but most
                                  teachers replied using TLN. Age was
                                  also a factor here, with younger
                                  teachers tending to use TLN, but
                                  some older ones, especially those
                                  holding senior posts, using FN.)
FN   Teachers

T/TLN   Teachers   (Teachers called students by FN,
                                  although they occasionally called
                                  boys by LN when angry. NN were
                                  more frequently used for boys, and
                                  by male teachers. Younger students
                                  tended to use titles – 'Sir/Miss' – more
                                  than older students who tended to
                                  use TLN.)
FN/NN/LN   Students

Activity

1   Write each of the abbreviations from the list above on a separate piece of card and turn them face downwards. With a partner select one card each at random. Work out a social context (or contexts) in which the two forms of address could be used by two people speaking to each other and say what respective power and status each would have. Reshuffle the cards and repeat the process until you have come up with several different combinations.

2   What are the different forms of address used *to you* in your school or

college? List them and write alongside what these forms of address tell you about your relationship with the person addressing you. Likely influences are relative status, age and gender.

3   Conduct a short survey of the non-teaching staff in your school or college, such as caretakers, secretaries, kitchen staff, etc., asking them how they are addressed by (a) the headteacher, (b) other senior staff, (c) teachers, (d) students. What does this tell you about the power relationships involved?

4   Walk round your institution and look at the various nameplates on office doors. What does the use of titles and names tell you about how the office owners are viewed by others, and possibly what they are wanting to say about themselves?

Power can be derived in a number of ways, and as shown above, power is reflected in language. Status, age and gender will all have been influences you detected at work as you examined naming conventions. A good starting point for looking at the language of sport and gender, therefore, is the use of a naming system, with the Wimbledon tennis tournament used as an example.

The Wimbledon tournament has conventions for how it names players on court. When umpires call the score, men are given no marital status and are referred to by surnames, i.e. 'Game and first set to Sampras'. Women, on the other hand, are given marital status and surname as in 'Advantage Miss Graf'.

This system is similar to that in conservative hierarchies where men address each other by surnames only. The All England Club at Wimbledon was, and in many ways still is, an elite institution. Such clubs were run by powerful, influential men who brought to sport the conventions of business and politics – men were called by surnames, women by marital status. Although this was an apparent sign of politeness to women, it in fact highlighted a difference in status, both in the roles of men and women and in the perception of the way they played. Use of surnames only gave a serious edge to competition, whereas polite titles made the women's game less important, more 'genteel'. Over the past thirty years women tennis players have campaigned hard for equality at Wimbledon. Those who have most actively done so have faced a barrage of hostility, especially from those sections of the media who wish to portray women in a way that focuses on their appearance and their expected gender characteristics.

An intricate pattern of naming is used by commentators and journalists which highlights the different ways men and women are perceived. When newspapers refer to tennis players, they are often called by their full name (Boris Becker) or by their surname (Becker). Women players, on the other hand, especially if they are famous, are often referred to by the more familiar use of first names (Martina, Conchita) or even shortened versions (Gabbi).

Newspaper reports also include **name tags**, a form of label which identifies well-known people and at the same time constructs a sense of the person's character or actions. These are particularly common in tabloid newspapers. In coverage of Wimbledon in 1995, Pete Sampras became 'Pistol Pete', while Andre Agassi was known as 'the Pirate of SW19' and 'the White Knight'.

These name tags often contain a good deal of assumed shared knowledge. 'Pistol Pete' referred, presumably, to the speed and accuracy of Sampras's play, his first name helping to make an **alliterative** effect. Agassi's name tags both referred in some way to his clothing, for which he was heavily sponsored. He was a pirate because of his headband (Wimbledon's address is London SW19), and a white knight because he agreed to change his coloured clothes for all-white kit. The connotative associations with whiteness and knight would suggest that we are meant to approve of Agassi as a person; he is chivalric and honourable in his approach to the game. Later he was called 'the white wizard', adding magical prowess to his considerable list of achievements.

You will notice that these tags are rooted in popular mythologies: Sampras, alias 'Pistol Pete', is a sharp-shooting cowboy; Agassi, alias a 'Pirate' and a 'White Knight', is both a buccaneer and a medieval warrior!

Women players are also given name tags, but from a different cultural source. Mary Pierce, who represents France, was called in one newspaper 'La Belle' and 'The Body' because of her 'slender and elegant build'. Another journalist even went so far as to say 'The Body, as she has been christened' thus claiming greater legitimacy for the invented name. Arantxa Sanchez-Vicario, on the other hand, was the 'Little Spaniard' and the 'Spanish Slugger'.

Activity

1   What connotations do you find with reference to the comments on the two women players mentioned above? How do they differ from the way the men are perceived?

2   Look in various newspapers for name tags which refer to sporting figures, both men and women. Explore the origins of these name tags and see whether gender plays a part in the way they are constructed. Tabloid newspapers, especially their headlines, are a particularly good source for this sort of data.

A trailer for radio coverage of Wimbledon in 1996 advertised that listeners would have a fortnight of 'Sun, serves and sex'. The reference to sex, supported by a clip from commentary of a women's match, contained language which reinforced the stereotype of the female athlete – tall, thin, long-legged, graceful.

At the time of Wimbledon 1995, Arantxa Sanchez-Vicario, the Spanish player referred to above, was 5ft 6ins tall and weighed 8st 12lbs. Mary Pierce was 5ft 11ins tall and weighed 9st 6lbs. Although Sanchez-Vicario was the more successful player, descriptions of her consistently referred to her failure to conform to the accepted stereotype of the female athlete.

Activity

Using the data below, taken from various newspaper reports of matches involving the two players, what pictures of the two players are constructed by the language used?

Mary Pierce

Her slow serve is a liability, but with her good looks and zillions in the bank, is that a problem?

She made a queenly entrance.

She is famous for having a figure ... The Body as she has been christened.

At least some of those present were more interested in her vital statistics than points won.

As elegantly and haughtily she struts from point to point.

She changed ends with a good deal of flouncing and head tossing.

On court she wears The Dress. She looks graceful in it, mind you; nobody is denying that.

Pierce signals a return to the notion that ladies glow.

If she were a chocolate drop she would eat herself.

Wimbledon's newest pin-up.

The crowd were impatient for their darling ... that most skilful and attractive woman.

She is a pretty ordinary player – or an ordinary pretty player.

22

Arantxa Sanchez-Vicario

The Spanish slugger who lumbers around the court.

The little Spaniard has an unlovely functionalism.

She looks like a schoolgirl that hates games.

She looks no more than a waitress scuffling around on her little legs.

She is a bit like Bambi - she is no formidable athlete.

The little dynamo.

She doesn't look like an athlete. Face pudgy, arms and legs the same.

Commentary

Sportswriters use a great deal of metaphorical language when describing sporting events, partly because they are giving an essentially static representation of a moving event. It is useful for a linguist to see how these metaphors combine to give an overall picture.

Mary Pierce is seen as regal — she makes 'a queenly entrance' and 'looks graceful'. She also moves 'elegantly and haughtily' while the suggestion that she 'struts' also carries a sense that she is distant and aloof, like a queen. This aloofness is further reinforced by the reference to her 'flouncing and head-tossing'.

At the same time as being aloof, she belongs to us all. She is 'the crowd's darling' but also their 'pin-up' whose 'vital statistics' concern her body shape, not her tennis ability to win points.

We are told that she has been 'christened The Body', presumably by journalists, but there is the implication that we are all happy to use that name. The capital letters in 'The Body' are repeated for its covering — 'The Dress'. The capital letters give emphasis to her body's importance and suggest that she has indeed been re-named, so that her body is her new and only identity.

A common metaphor for sexual attraction involves food and eating. Women are often described as food — 'tart', 'crumpet', they are 'dishy', 'tasty '; if women are food then they can be consumed by hungry men. Here there is the suggestion of Pierce being a chocolate drop, although the writer perhaps acknowledges the extravagance of the suggestion by saying 'If she were a chocolate drop'. The conclusion to this, that she would eat herself, suggests that her desirability is enhanced by her being unattainable.

23

Pierce is described as both a woman and a lady. Sanchez-Vicario, though, is 'a schoolgirl', 'a Spaniard' and a 'waitress'. The last two are probably linked; the Spanish waiter (as with Manuel in *Fawlty Towers*) is itself a stereotypical role and so an easy point of reference for the writer.

The words which describe Pierce's movement suggest proportion, grace. Sanchez-Vicario, however 'lumbers' and 'scuffles' on her 'little legs'. These words paint a picture of awkwardness that does not conform to the expected female sporting stereotype.

She is also a 'slugger', in other words she hits the ball hard, a necessary ability for a tennis player. The word 'slugger', though, carries connotations of clumsiness and heavy-handedness. Her failure to *look* like an athlete is a constant point of reference; she is 'pudgy', she is 'Bambi'. Just as women are sometimes compared to food, so they are often compared to animals, via terms such as 'bitch', 'cow'. Sanchez-Vicario is in contrast to the thoroughbred Pierce who tosses her head like a racehorse.

She is also 'unlovely', the gravest of all sins for the female sports player. At first sight this negative may appear to be a slightly weaker form of the word 'ugly', but in fact it shows the real nature of Sanchez-Vicario's offence; in being 'unlovely', she is not living up to the required stereotype. In the journalists' eyes she is failing to fit into the accepted **ideology** which governs the sports pages. Similarly her energy and stamina are referred to in the word 'dynamo' – a machine-like quality rather than a truly human attribute. This is also implied by the reference to her 'functionalism'.

So, on the one hand we have images of grace, queenliness, on the other an unlovely automaton. Yet it was Sanchez-Vicario who proved herself to be far the more successful tennis player, which was, after all, the real point of the exercise.

Activity

Text: Mary Pierce is a newspaper description of Mary Pierce. Rewrite the extract, replacing Mary Pierce with the name of a male player, and then changing all the pronouns from female to male. What effect is created by doing this, and what does it tell you about the language of the original article?

24

Text: Mary Pierce

Glamorous Mary Pierce cruised through her first round clash and promised a brand new outfit – but not until the US Open.

Pierce was a sensation at the French Open with her all-black number, but at Wimbledon she wore a demure all-white outfit. All the same, it gave the packed centre court plenty of opportunity to appreciate her shapely contours as she contemptuously swept aside her opponent.

From the very first point, her long legs glided across the court as though she was on ice. With her blond hair tied back, and her classical features unblemished by as much as a bead of perspiration, she advanced coolly into round two.

Pierce said 'The outfit I wore today is the one I'm going to be wearing for Wimbledon. It is appropriate for this tournament – very classical and very simple'.

Running commentaries

The second sport to be looked at in this chapter is athletics, which also has male and female participants at the same overall event. The data in this section is taken from the 1995 World Championships in Gothenburg. In the section on tennis we saw men portrayed as either real people or mythological heroes, whereas women were either sexually available bodies or unlovely machines. This emphasis on the body is given even greater legitimation in athletics partly through the fact that the costumes the athletes wear are more streamlined and so accentuate their bodies more. This section will show how various features of the human body are focused on in athletics commentaries.

Merlene Ottey, the female sprinter, was referred to five times in one race as 'the tall slim figure'. The Swedish male athlete Patrick Joubert, who is unusually tall, was referred to as 'the very tall thin figure'. At first glance it appears as though both are being described in much the same way. There is, though, a difference. The word 'figure' has a number of meanings. Among these are a person, a shape, a representation (as in 'figure of fun' or 'figurehead'). With regards to women only, though, it refers to physical shape and attributes linked to sexual desirability.

When the word 'figure' is applied to Joubert it simply identifies him as a person, without any sense of sexual attractiveness. The word 'thin' describes his physical shape, and no more than this. When applied to

Ottey, though, the words 'tall' and 'slim' carry sexual associations, especially when used alongside the word 'figure'. 'Thin' for a woman signifies being underweight and so unattractive, whereas 'slim' means pleasingly thin, attractively so. 'Slim' carries positive connotations for women, something they are supposed to aspire to – a degree of thinness pleasing to men.

Hair colour can work in the same way. There were many more references to women's hair than to men's in the data collected from the World Championships, the most common being to blonde hair. Some typical examples were;

> the blonde haired Slovenian
>
> a slight blonde haired figure
>
> a tall slim figure with blonde hair
>
> the tall blonde haired Dutch woman

Blonde hair on women is associated with sexual attractiveness, as in the case of film stars such as Marilyn Monroe. Although there were occasional references to men's hair, such as 'the tall, long blond haired Swede Joubert', it was the length of hair and a stereotypical Swedish blondness which were the focus of attention. There is no sense here that sexual attractiveness is being referred to.

The most common word applied to men's physique was 'big'. It was used over thirty times during one day's television coverage. References to women were more specific and tended to name actual features, especially their legs. Legs, of course, are a vital part of the athlete's body, but they are also a key component of one stereotypical view of the ideal woman – slim figure, blonde hair, long shapely legs.

Some examples from television coverage of women's events are:

> those long legs
>
> those long legs reach for the sand
>
> the long legs are really eating up the track
>
> those powerful legs
>
> with the length of her legs

Long legs, like blonde hair, form part of the stereotypically attractive female athlete. As there is no similar stereotype for men, the much less specific 'big' does enough of a job, because it refers to athletic strength and power, not sexual attractiveness. The word 'big' applied to a female athlete would carry very different connotations.

Leading ladies

There were some interesting differences in the way athletes' personal lives were commented on. On ten occasions a leading female athlete's husband and marriage were referred to. Some examples are:

> Torrance, now thirty, married to her coach has a son Manly, he's now 5 years old.

> She then moved to Spain where she's married.

> She subsequently married the Italian pole-vault record holder.

> ... married to her coach Manly Walker good sprinter himself ...

With regard to women athletes, it seems that marriage is in itself important enough to mention without further detail needed. It is as though women have an inferred status that is only fully realised through their role relationships with men. They have no status of their own. Those women athletes who have no male partner cause a particular problem to journalists who cannot place them in a convenient category. Because of this they are often treated with considerable suspicion.

There were fewer references to men's private lives, but two typical ones were:

> Well I'm sure his wife Alison and his sons will be watching this.

> His wife Steph in Leeds and his young son will be rooting for him now.

Here you will notice that the wife and children will be supporting the husband, that the main focus of the statements is the man's performance. When the British athlete Yvonne Graham ran, she was referred to as the wife of Winthrop Graham. When Winthrop ran, no mention was made of his wife.

Activity

Text: Hockey is taken from a profile, of the hockey player Jane Sixsmith. The main headline of the article was 'On red alert for Atlanta' and a second headline described her as 'The Leading Lady of British Hockey'. It was written by Simon Hogan and published in the *Independent On Sunday*.

Text: Hockey

Other teams may play with more flair – the Koreans, for example – and some may have the resources to go about things more professionally, notably Australia, who as world champions are one of three teams automatically assured of a place at next year's Olympics along with the hosts, the United States, and the Olympic champions, Spain. But for fighting qualities, Britain stand comparison with anyone else in the world, and nobody embodies this spirit better than the 28-year-old Sixsmith, the red-headed striker whose 40 goals in 98 internationals – she has played another 101 times for England – have helped make Britain a force in the game.

It was an irony, therefore, that of the 10 goals Britain scored in South Africa, not one of them came from the formidable stick of Sixsmith. "To be honest I didn't feel I had many chances," she said. "But I wasn't disappointed in that I assisted with many of the goals."

Such is Sixsmith's stature, however, that just having her on the field is a source of immeasurable strength to the team. "She's feared by opponents, and she's also greatly respected by our own players," Sue Slocombe, the Great Britain coach, said. "She's worth her weight in gold

from that point of view. She's a real stalwart. Her work-rate is absolutely tremendous. She grafts as much when we don't have the ball as when we do, so that's an added dimension in a striker's game."

On a grey autumn afternoon, in the office at the Birmingham Sports Centre where after her South African adventure she was back working as an assistant coaching co-ordinator for the city council, Sixsmith seemed to radiate energy all the more warmly. She used to do work in the council's payroll department until it occurred to them that it might be to everyone's advantage for her to have a job in sport. It suits Sixsmith perfectly – there are training facilities on hand, and the council are good about giving her time off to play.

Sixsmith is a Brummie through and through – born and brought up in Sutton Coldfield, where she still lives with her husband, Tim, and plays for the local club, Sutton Canada Life. She first represented Great Britain in 1988, in the series of play-off matches from which they qualified for the Seoul Olympics. That was the year that Britain's men's hockey team, Sean Kerly et al, became Olympic champions, following the bronze they had won in Los Angeles in 1984. The

women's team had to wait until 1992 for their first taste of glory when Sixsmith's goals helped them bring home an unexpected bronze medal.

Just as the men had hoped, the women saw this as the start of something big for the game as a whole. But it didn't happen. "I don't think we built on the success we had," Sixsmith said. "We could have attracted sponsors. The BBC offered us coverage but the association said it wasn't the right time of year, whereas if they'd asked us players we'd have jumped at it. I think they were a bit naïve." Still even Sixsmith adheres to the basic truth about hockey – that it is a better game to play than to watch.

After Atlanta, her third Olympic Games, Sixsmith says she will almost certainly retire from international hockey. So what chance of her doing so in possession of another bronze medal, or perhaps even better? World-wide, speed and fitness levels are increasing fast. Britain's approach is much more thorough than it was, but with all non-Olympic international hockey played by the individual home nations, opportunities for the larger grouping to get together are limited. "The spirit and will to win are very strong," Sixsmith said. And, after all, it takes only two seconds to score a goal.

Read the article carefully and, in groups if possible, prepare responses to the following questions.

1   A number of words and phrases describe the qualities of Jane Sixsmith's play. Can they be grouped into a semantic field?
2   What reference is made to her appearance and to her life outside hockey? Say whether you think these details add usefully to the profile.
3   What references are made to men in this article? What effect do they have on the overall focus of the article?
4   Do you think the article constructs a picture of a woman sports player in a different way from how men are usually portrayed?

Text: Hockey has been chosen because it does not show the obvious sort of treatment you might expect to find if you were reading a tabloid news-paper. It is certainly possible, though, to find here some features which are typical of the way female sports players are represented by the media.

There are many words and phrases which suggest that Sixsmith plays with strength and determination: she 'embodies fighting qualities'; her stature (which could refer to her physique or her reputation) is a 'source of strength' to others in the team; she is 'feared by opponents', and is 'a real stalwart'; 'her work-rate is tremendous' and 'she grafts'. There is also reference to her 'formidable stick', endowing a piece of equipment, her hockey stick, with a quality of her play.

In addition there are references to her age, her hair colour (she is called 'red-headed'), her job where she is said to 'radiate energy', where she lives and to the fact that she lives with her husband.

Men, in addition to her husband, are referred to in a number of ways. There are references to Britain's men's team and to a famous male player, Sean Kerly. Women's hopes for more media coverage are compared to men's in the phrase 'Just as the men had hoped'. If we assume that the senior council staff are largely male, then it is they who suggest a change of job.

In the opening headline she is described as 'a leading lady'. A 'leading lady' is an old-fashioned term for an actress, and the word 'lady' itself now carries associations of condescension and inequality. 'Golden attribute' may refer to Olympic success but also has a sense of her

29

appearance and hair colour. Although the language describing her qualities of strength and determination could equally be applied to men, it is unlikely that a man would be called 'red-headed'.

The reference to her husband seems unnecessary – nothing else is made of it – but is perhaps included to let us know that she actually has a husband and so is heterosexual. The men's hockey team is seen as more successful than the women's, and her celebrity status has to be placed alongside Sean Kerly, whose fame is taken for granted. It is the council, not Sixsmith herself, who find the most suitable job for her.

This article, then, although not obviously stereotypical, nonetheless constructs within a framework of a male-dominated world a picture of Sixsmith in terms of her appearance and her sexuality. Her success can only be affirmed alongside that of men and it is men who have contributed to it.

A similar effect can be seen in a profile of heptathlete Denise Lewis which appeared in the *Independent* before the Atlanta Olympic games in 1996. Lewis is described as 'one of the most striking pin-ups . . . who has the looks to maximise the commercial possibilities of greater projection'. In addition we are told that 'comparisons with Daley Thompson are hardly appropriate'. Hardly appropriate perhaps, but they are made nonetheless.

The language used to describe men and women in sport illustrates some of the ways in which men and women are viewed differently in our society. Naming systems reflect different social attitudes to gender, while because sport involves physical activity, references to bodies are especially frequent. While such references to male physique relate to sporting prowess only, those to female physique relate as much to sexuality as to sport. Female sports players are often represented as part of a male world, with males guiding and helping their performance.

Extension

1   Profiles of sports players often appear in newspapers before a major sporting event. Collect some of these, including some about women. You will find these particularly before tennis and athletics tournaments, as these are two sports for which women receive most coverage.

Research the ways in which women and men are presented, looking in particular for differences that have been discussed in this unit. These include:

◎   The way they are named, including name tags and nicknames
◎   References to physical shape and appearance
◎   Their relationships with partners
◎   Any other interesting patterns of language use that you can
      detect

2   Although coverage of women's sport remains limited on television
     and radio, there are now more events which would allow you to
     collect comparative data. In addition to tennis and athletics, golf is
     another sport which could provide interesting data.

         Equestrianism, on the other hand, is rare in that men and
     women compete on equal terms against each other. Commentary
     on show jumping and eventing could provide material for an
     investigation into gender and sport.

The state of the game

To understand how sport is represented to the public, you need to look at the language that is used and the values and associations which come with that language. In doing this you will gain a greater understanding of sport's place in society and how it reflects the values that society holds.

One way in which sport is represented is through ideas surrounding national identity. In sports where the contest is between individuals, the performance of the individual is often represented in terms of a national personality stereotype. A good example to look at here is how Swedish sports players are described; Sweden has produced many outstanding tennis players, golfers and footballers in recent times. The essential stereotype of the Swede involves coolness, calmness, psychological strength. The first Swedish tennis player to make his mark internationally was Bjorn Borg; he was often referred to as 'The Iceberg' and, in a pun on his name, 'Ice Borg'. The Swedish golfer Jesper Parnevik is often described as having 'a cool frame of mind'. The origin of this stereotype may in part reflect a view of the Swedish climate and landscape, rather than any scientifically proven psychological facts, but the stereotype is strong enough to be seen in sports coverage throughout Europe. Like all stereotypes, though, even when apparently favourable, it has a negative side to it; to be cool and mentally strong undoubtedly helps when playing sport, but the stereotype also carries connotations of dullness, of lack of emotion, of boring functionalism.

National teams are just as likely to be viewed stereotypically. The stereotype attached to German teams involves discipline, reliability, teamwork and efficiency – many of the qualities said to belong to German manufacturing. The German football team, therefore, is said to 'steamroller' the opposition, and they are often described as 'a machine', a machine which runs smoothly and efficiently to victory. Top German individuals are described in the same terms, such as the tennis players Graf and Becker. They 'grind their opponents down' while their service has 'a machine-like efficiency'.

The dominant British stereotype presented abroad – usually spoken of in terms of Englishness – involves courage, commitment and fighting spirit. At times of high sporting excitement, and some national success, the same stereotype appears in British sports coverage too, suggesting that stereotypes are not exclusively about attitudes to foreigners. They are also used within the nation itself, providing, that is, that there are positive features to be found, features which can give a sense of national identity and well-being.

Activity

Research coverage of sports involving individuals or teams from particular countries and/or continents. (The list below offers some possibilities, although the ones you choose may well depend upon what events are taking place at the time.) What stereotypical portayal of a nation/continent can you detect in the coverage?

France, Italy, Germany, South America, Africa, Australia

The sporting battlefield

National stereotypes are often expressed in metaphorical terms; the cool Swede, the mechanical German, the lion-hearted British. Sporting contests, tactics and skills are also described in metaphorical terms and one of the most obvious fields of reference for sporting metaphor is that of war. Some of these metaphors are so deeply embedded in the way that we describe sport, that we fail to notice them consciously as metaphors.

In football, for instance, we refer to 'attack and defence'. The attack 'shoots' for goal, and the 'shot' can be 'off target' or 'on target'. When the game is drawn, it is decided by a decisive penalty 'shoot-out'. The opponents often 'defend enemy territory', and 'raiders break out of defence' in an attempt to 'attack the opposition's rearguard'. A

34

particularly sharp break-out is 'a counter-attack'. A sustained spell of attack will lead to 'a siege' of the opponents' line.

The word 'volley', meaning an aggressive shot, is used a great deal in football and tennis. The word derives from the Latin *volare*, meaning 'to fly', and was used to describe a fierce attack of first arrows and then artillery in battle. In its military sense it involves a large number of shots, but when used in sport it refers to one shot only, but a particularly fierce and effective one. This ferocity comes from the fact that the ball has not been allowed to bounce – the volley is itself taken 'on the volley', still in flight.

The sports media use many references to war in their coverage of events. Typical examples taken from a range of sports covered by a newspaper on one day included:

The England cricketers battled their way back into the match.

The French athlete intends to defend her title.

The Belgian rider fought off a strong challenge in the Tour de France.

In international competition metaphors of war appear most frequently when the media can equate the sporting contest with actual wars which have taken place between the countries. In Euro 96 England played both Scotland and Germany. The United Kingdom, on sporting occasions, is sometimes one country (as in the Olympic Games) and at other times four separate countries. Whenever England play Scotland in a major event, the talk is inevitably of war. When the teams met in Euro 96, media from both countries evoked the spirit of ancient battlefield clashes. An English newspaper report on the game, won by England, described how England 'put Scotland to the sword in this Battle of Britain', in the process mixing allusions to different wars. By the time England played Germany, the coverage in many newspapers was expressed in terms of all-out war (see Text: Stuart Pearce).

Such descriptions are not confined to international sport. Within nations there are regional divides which can be expressed through sport; Barcelona *v.* Madrid in Spain, North *v.* South in England and Italy. These are particularly strong when the rivalry is accompanied by political and/ or economic differences between the regions.

Activity

1 Select two popular sports and write down the well-known meta-phorical terms used in them to describe tactics, playing area, players, moves, positions, etc. In a larger group, if possible, pool your ideas and see whether the metaphors belong to any common fields of meaning. Look in particular for metaphors associated with war and battle.

2 Look at the sports coverage of newspapers over a few days. (You will find that broadsheets are likely to have a wider range of coverage.) Collect as many examples as you can of metaphors derived from war.

Text: Stuart Pearce from the *Sun* newspaper appeared the day before England played football against Germany in the Euro 96 competition. Newspapers for a number of days had previewed the match which was seen as a particularly significant one; not only was it a semi-final, but it repeated previous close encounters between the two nations. Additionally it allowed the tabloid press to recall the Second World War. They did so by simplifying this war, implying that it had been a straight fight between England and Germany, a fight that England had won.

The article appeared on the front and second pages of the newspaper, outside the normal sports pages. It focused on the England player Stuart Pearce, because after he had missed a vital penalty in the 1990 game with Germany he scored with one against Spain in the previous round of Euro 96.

Activity

Read the article carefully and write notes on the following:

1 What metaphors of war and fighting are used?
2 How is the idea of national identity developed?
3 Using ideas explored in Unit 2, what role is played by Pearce's wife in the story that is constructed by this article?

Text: Stuart Pearce

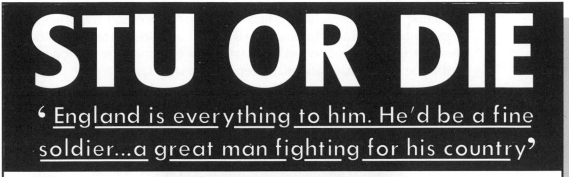

STU OR DIE

' England is everything to him. He'd be a fine soldier...a great man fighting for his country'

EXCLUSIVE

By JOHN ASKILL

ENGLAND lionheart Stuart Pearce would be proud to DIE for his country, his devoted wife said last night.

Liz Pearce told how her hubby keys himself up for battle before matches – and spoke of the fearless fighting spirit that spurs him on to victory.

She told The Sun exclusively: "It's not just a case of playing for his country, Stuart wants to **WIN** for his country.

"He would make a good soldier, a great person to have fighting for us. If ever he went to war, and every soldier had the same passion for his country as Stuart, we could never lose.

"England means everything to him. The roar of 'England, England' at Wembley on Saturday was just incredible. It was everything Stuart loves and everything he could dream of. Just watch him before the kick-off against Germany – nobody will sing the National Anthem with so much passion.

"Nothing would make him more proud than winning Euro 96 for England."

Attractive blonde Liz, 34, who wed the Nottingham Forest star five years ago, went on: "He is just so patriotic.

"I bought him a 25 ft flagpole complete with Union Jack one Christmas and he said it was the best present he ever had.

"I will never meet anyone else who has so much courage and guts. He is so full of drive.

"When he stepped up to take that penalty against Spain, I could hardly watch.

"I could see all the determination and tension in his face. It meant the whole world to him.

"He was shouting at the crowd, encouraging them to lift themselves even further.

Proved

"But then he turned to me in the stands, where I was sitting with my brothers, raised his fist and gave me a shout."

Liz was also watching that fateful 1990 World Cup semi-final where Stuart missed a penalty against Germany.

She said: "When he came home he used to watch the video of the match, especially the penalty shootout, over and over again.

"We didn't really talk about it for a long time but then he was full of, 'if onlys'. He kept saying, 'I should have lifted it. It should have gone higher'.

"He suffered dreadfully. Sometimes fans would say something to him when we were out – either blaming him for England being eliminated or saying that he shouldn't worry

"Either way it wouldn't go away. But perhaps it will after that penalty on Saturday.

"When the ball went into the net it was as if he had waited six years for that moment."

Liz revealed: "Stuart gets a kick out of being scared, so I wasn't surprised when he stepped up to take the penalty. I knew in my heart he would not turn it down.

"When we went on holiday to America, all he wanted to do was get on the biggest and scariest rollercoaster he could find.

"That is probably where he gets his 'Psycho' name from fans. He likes to beat his own fear.

"The best present he could ever give me in his life would be to phone me from the England camp and tell me that he will not take another penalty in a shootout.

"If he would just call to say, 'I've done it. I have proved I can do it. I have got over it all now and I don't need to do it again'.

"He didn't have to prove it to anybody – only to himself. Well, he's done that now so he could say, 'Never again'. But I know he won't. There could be two more matches and two more shootouts.

"Stuart is brave enough and his heart is big enough to step up both times and I know he will."

Olympic ideals

One view of language is that it shapes the way we see things, rather than reflecting what we see. (This is known as the Sapir-Whorf hypothesis, named after two American linguists.) If sport is described in terms of war, then perhaps that is how we view it - a far cry from the dictionary definition of recreation and play referred to in Unit 1.

The British runner Kelly Holmes was described under a newspaper photograph as 'Representing Queen and Country' at the Atlanta Olympics. Part of the language here no doubt refers to the fact that she is in the army, but all the same, there is a sense of the athlete going off to fight for her country rather than run in a race.

The reality of Olympic competition is very different from the ideals that the Olympic movement still exhibits in its ceremonies. Baron Pierre de Coubertin, the founder of the modern Olympics, was inspired by the ancient Greek ideal of the harmony between body and mind, albeit the male body and mind. (He described women athletes as 'a very unedifying spectacle'.) He believed that the new Olympic movement would allow men from all over the world to compete in a spirit of friendship which would lead to world peace and understanding. The famous words which make up the Olympic ideal come not from de Coubertin, though, but from Bishop Ethelbert Talbot from Pennsylvania, who, during a sermon in St Paul's Cathedral before the London Olympics of 1908 said: 'The important thing in the Olympic games is less to win than to take part ... The essential thing is not to have conquered but to have fought well.' Even the ideal, you will note, draws upon a metaphor of war for its expression.

The most famous example of sport being used to promote nationalism and national identity is the Olympic Games of 1936 in Berlin. Hitler's attempt to turn the games into a Nazi celebration was partly overshadowed by the success of the black runner Jesse Owens, who won four gold medals. In more recent times political concerns have led to boycotts of the Moscow games in 1980 and retaliation by the former communist countries in boycotting the Los Angeles games in 1984.

These very obvious manifestations of national identity over-shadowing 'the Olympic ideal' sometimes obscure the fact that all Olympic competition is covered by the media in a nationalistic way. Each nation follows most closely its own winners, with commentators using phrases like 'it's gold for Britain' as a way of linking the nation with an individual's success. If individual success leads to national rejoicing, then collective failure can lead to recrimination. The failure of British athletes in the 1996 Atlanta Olympics was seen as evidence of national decline and led to enquiries into the spiritual as well as physical health of the nation. After the 1994 Football World Cup a Colombian player was shot dead on his return from the tournament for playing a major role in his country's defeat.

The sprinter Frankie Fredericks, who comes from Namibia in Southern Africa said before the Atlanta Olympics, 'I'm not doing this sport to be famous. I look at it as an opportunity to put my country on the map'. Many countries have invested hugely in sport, using it as a means to promote internal unity and world recognition. In apartheid South Africa, large sums of money were spent on the whites' traditional games of rugby and cricket, in an attempt to play international sport. The claim was that sport lies outside politics, whereas in fact sport was being used in an attempt to gain international political recognition. Yet Nelson Mandela, when visiting a cricket match in Soweto said, 'Sport has a role to play in the uniting of many countries of the world because it speaks a language far beyond the reach of politicians'. The suggestion that sport lies outside the world of politics, that it speaks a language of its own, is in fact a very political statement. The fact that both sides of a political divide used much the same argument, albeit for different purposes, shows that the language which sport speaks is no different from any other language; it is part of the social and political fabric of nations.

Sporting legends

The following two texts take a different approach to sport, challenging some of the stereotypes of nationhood that have been seen so far.

Both are about cricket. The connotations of that game, as seen in Unit 1, make it a game which is strongly associated with England and a certain view of Englishness. This is likely to be reflected and reinforced by the media, especially when circumstances allow, as they did when the England captain Mike Atherton batted for two days to avoid defeat and to secure a draw against South Africa. The first Text, by Robert Winder in the *Independent*, was in the newspaper's analysis section rather than its sports pages.

Winder describes how other newspapers had covered the story, making connections between the language they used and a view of English history based on two things: warfare and the way that warfare has been mythologised by various texts, including film.

A very English hero

Michael Atherton's heroics had the nation's males swooning. What makes him a 'lionheart'? Robert Winder explains ...

Michael Atherton's match-saving innings in Johannesburg was by any standards a historic feat: one of the most distinguished and brave performances by an England captain – or any player – ever. So it is not surprising that the "nation" as newspapers like to call themselves these days, has indulged in a frenzy of praise. The *Sun* and the *Mirror* spoke with one voice: "Arise Sir Mike!" Even the serious papers spoke of "medals for valour", "bravery under fire" and the spirit of Rorke's Drift: one could see them imagining Atherton as Michael Caine in the movie, repelling the Zulu asault with nothing more than a boyish expression, a smart red-coat and a motionless upper lip.

The verdict was unanimous: Mike Atherton was an utter hero – in the best English sense of the word: his defiance in the face of almost certain defeat was an epic instance of our favourite sporting virtue: bloody mindedness.

It would have been better if he'd been hit a few more times – bloody headbands are good news on such occasions. But the word "staunch" kept cropping up on the radio commentary, and the papers were full of that's-the-spirit epithets evoking heroics on battlefields past: Atherton was "lion-hearted"; he had shown "valour over the call of duty".

It was indeed a great performance. But it was, in particular, an innings guaranteed to appeal to an English audience. There are two guiding national fantasies when it comes to great sporting prowess.

First there is our love of Great Escapes – everything from Dunkirk to Colditz and the Wood Horse. More important, there is our unswerving devotion to never-say-die heroics, to the dogged they-shall-not-pass spirit we perhaps fear that we possess no more.

It isn't a coincidence that both of these myths derive from the Second World War, just as it isn't a coincidence that England's overseas fan club calls itself the "Barmy Army". The *Sun* tried a few sporting metaphors for Atherton's feat, explaining that his innings was "an Everest of concentration". But these seemed pretty thin stuff besides the hectic volleys of martial acclaim. It was a "rearguard action"; he had proved himself "in the white heat of conflict"; he and his partner Jack Russell ran off the field "comrades in arms".

This kind of language and the ease with which it is lapped up is a familiar modern echo of the tub thumped by Churchill during the war; the few defying the many, a tiny country punching above its weight against mighty hordes of incomprehensible and probably hostile foreigners. We thrill to the idea of a small band of heroes trapped in a stockade, holding out against vicious odds.

Atherton's long day in the South Africa sun deserves the wildest praise. But this sort of praise is indeed wild. The ironic part is that the virtue we like to think as typically English – bulldog spit-in-your eye defiance – has become as rare as English victories. Our cricket team has shown, in recent years, a near suicidal tendency to collapse when the wind blows hard. At times the attitude seemed to be that if you couldn't win, you might as well lose fast so you could watch the golf on the telly. But Atherton won't need anyone to remind him to take the acclaim with the same ironic determination required to survive the equally hysterical abuse he has been exposed to.

He will know, even if the papers conveniently forget it, that he nearly made a pig's ear of the match by misreading the wicket and letting South Africa bat first. Again, if he had been caught at short leg at 99, it would have been another definite failure. On such delicate threads of circumstance hang sporting reputations.

1   In this article there are many references to (a) metaphors of war, (b) historical events, (c) fictional representations of history. In groups, if possible, list as many of these references as you can. Don't worry if you are unsure about some of the historical detail.
2   In the light of the evidence you found in (1) what point is Winder making about the contribution of sport to national identity?

Commentary

The headline 'A very English hero' immediately identifies that Winder is focusing on the idea that there are special qualities for a hero who is 'English'. The use of the **modifier** 'very', meaning absolute/total, gives a sense of possible over-statement and thus alerts the reader to the fact that the headline could be ironic in intention. This is developed later in the article when Atherton is called 'an utter hero – in the best English sense of the word'; the English sense involving facing defeat rather than chasing victory.

Among the many general associations made with war are 'medals for valour', 'bravery under fire', 'valour over the call of duty', 'they-shall-not-pass', 'rearguard action', 'comrades in arms'. There is a sense in all of these of a man deserving official recognition for his bravery – presumably the Victoria Cross.

'Arise, Sir Mike' is a reference to Queen Elizabeth I knighting Francis Drake after he had circumnavigated the world – not strictly a military success, but with the most common association with Drake being his victory over the Spanish Armada, the connection is made. Rorke's Drift was a battle in the Zulu Wars – a defeat for the English (actually British) army, but a legendary display of courage, as shown in the film *Zulu*. Describing Atherton as lion-hearted echoes Richard the Lion-Heart, a medieval crusader, and is also an oblique reference to the England badge which contains a lion.

The 'small band of heroes trapped in a stockade' is a more oblique reference, probably to the sieges of the Boer War, such as Mafeking. The test match was played in South Africa, and the Relief of Mafeking was a rescue rather than a victory – just like the test match.

References to the fictional accounts of war include *Zulu*; the film *The Great Escape* (the use of capital letters in the phrase 'our love of Great Escapes' is a clue here); the television series *Colditz* which dramatised escapes from the German prison; and *The Wooden Horse* (here called the Wood Horse, perhaps a misprint) which was a novel and then a film based on a famous escape in the Second World War.

Winder shows that an image of nationhood is constructed out of a mixture of history, myth and fiction. Sport both draws on the image for its frames of reference and reinforces it by its use of language. When he talks of 'our unswerving devotion to never-say-die heroics ... that we perhaps fear that we possess no more' he is saying that cricket, often known as the 'national game', is being used to bolster a myth of Englishness that is losing its potency even as a myth. In other words there is more to sport than a mere game.

He undermines this reporting of sport by implying that the newspapers he refers to have gone over the top in their praise of Atherton. He says that sporting reputation hangs on 'delicate threads of circumstance' – luck in other words – and that the media coverage would have been as hostile had England lost as it is laudatory because the match was saved. The increasingly vitriolic abuse of sports players and national teams who lose – and Atherton himself received such abuse both before this game and soon after it – reflects the fact that sport has to provide the raw material for national myth and identity now that military action cannot. Significantly, the *Sun* newspaper, which created the motto 'The paper that supports our boys' during the Falklands War, knowingly resurrected it before the semi-final of Euro 96, with the words 'The paper that genuinely supports our boys'.

The second article comes from a relatively new form of sports writing, the fanzine. Fanzines challenge the alliance between sport and the media, an alliance which reinforces the various stereotypes, including those of national identity, as shown by Robert Winder above. The word 'fanzine' is a **blend word** of 'fan', itself a short form of 'fanatic', and 'magazine'. Fanzines, then, are written by supporters of the game, people who have traditionally been ignored in sport's power structures. Fanzines take a much less respectful view of sport and challenge some of the typical stereotypes. That is why they are often banned from club shops and frequently receive little encouragement from the sports of which their writers are fans.

Activity

Text: Sri Lanka, slightly edited, appeared in the cricket fanzine *JM96**. At the time it was written in 1995, England had consistently refused to play an international against Sri Lanka. Sri Lanka went on to win the cricket World Cup in 1996.

What are the linguistic methods used by Mark Steel in this article to confront and challenge some of the traditional stereotypes of English cricket?

FRED'S A RIGHT SRI LANKA

The Mark Steel Solution

"It's bloody outrageous", I'm sure MCC members must be complaining. "Sri Lanka were allowed Test status because once India and Pakistan were better than us there was no team we could call "Funny little chaps; bloody hopeless but wonderfully entertaining"'.

Some must be even more enraged at their latest victory against Pakistan. For instance Fred Trueman. Most people by now must know that the country's name is pronounced 'Shree', or 'Sree' Lanka, but never Srie (rhyming with pie) Lanka. Most people however do not have the benefit, as Fred has of having sat in commentary boxes for five days at a time hearing a variety of colleagues pronounce 'Sri Lanka' correctly every time they told the score. But like a child mischievously saying 'Bum' in front of a granny, Fred draws a breath each time he approaches the word and with relish says it – 'Srie Lanka'.

Why are there no plans for Sri Lanka to have a full Test series against England? They have now beaten most other countries in at least one Test, including England so they can hardly be considered unworthy opponents.

Maybe it could be argued that as none of their players are known the tickets would be hard to sell. But apart from the fact that they aren't likely to become known while confined to the 'other sport' section beneath the volleyball in the broadsheets, this didn't seem to apply to South Africa's unknown team when they returned to test status.

The sad truth is that Sri Lanka's battle for credibility with English cricket authorities is another example of the stripey tie brigade's belief in the natural order. We may have been soundly thrashed by everyone for the last ten years but now we've drawn with someone so order is restored and, as John Thicknesse in the London Evening Standard said, that makes us ready to resume our place as the world's greatest cricketing nation.

The attitude to the fact that the last time we played Sri Lanka we lost is like the bloke in a pub who loses at pool to a woman. 'Ha ha, yeah well done love, course I was only mucking about like, so it er don't really count. Right lads, now who wants a proper game!'

That way we don't have to trouble ourselves with playing those funny, if entertaining little chaps from 'What's it called these days?'

JM96

Commentary

The starting point for fanzines is that the authors and readers share a good deal of detailed knowledge of the sport. References do not need to be explained. It is expected that the reader knows who Fred Trueman is (a former player now broadcaster) and that he has a reputation for conservatism, for thinking that the modern game is not as good as it was in his playing days.

The headline uses techniques similar to those of tabloid journalism – it uses the first name 'Fred' on the assumption we recognise the name, and it uses a form of rhyming slang to put across its viewpoint. For 'Sri Lanka' read 'wanker'. The MCC is an elite, all-male club which owns Lord's cricket ground and which has a big influence on the game. Steel caricatures its members as being conservative and racist. Not only is the old order changing, but as far as the MCC is concerned, 'funny little chaps' from Sri Lanka are beginning to win games. Later in the article the MCC members are called 'the stripey tie brigade', a reference to the tie they wear in their exclusive Lord's pavilion. Wearing a tie, particularly a striped one, is equated with being outdated and reactionary.

Steel ridicules Trueman as a conservative and a bigot. His refusal to pronounce Sri Lanka correctly is typical of cricket commentators who claim to have problems with Asian names. During the India tour of 1996, radio and television commentators made repeated reference to Indian players' names. Ganguly, a player who went on to score a century in his first test, was particularly a figure of so-called fun. This was because his name, within an English context of sound and meaning, can be likened to boy scout songs (gin gan gooly) and to sexual innuendo (goolies). In fact his Bengali name means 'sweet smell', but this was not commented upon. (The broadcaster Sue Lawley, when reading the news in the 1980s, said 'I cannot possibly pronounce the name of the bowler who has taken eight wickets against England'. His name was Shrivaramakrishnan, a combination of the names of three Hindu gods (Shiva–Rama–Krishna). It is in fact perfectly easy for any English speaker to say, and anyway she would have been given advice by the BBC Pronunciation Unit. Her difficulty with the word was clearly pre-arranged and scripted.)

Because of the assumed shared knowledge, much of the language in the article works by ironic implication. The reference to South Africa is an example of this. South Africa returned to test cricket after the dismantling of apartheid, but throughout the years of their ban, English touring teams played white-only sides. Cricket lovers would know that these illegal tours were supported by many in the cricketing hierarchy and that the South African team is still mainly white. Steel implies that

44

the reasons for refusing to play Sri Lanka, therefore, are racial in origin.

He ironically mocks the view that England is 'the world's greatest cricketing nation' by contrasting it with with the fact (albeit slightly exaggerated) that 'we have been soundly thrashed by everyone'.

His reference to 'the bloke in the pub' who is unable to accept defeat by the supposedly inferior woman mocks the cricket establishment in two ways. The woman who can play pool is equivalent to the Sri Lankans who can play cricket; both show a prowess that cannot be acknowledged because they belong to a stereotypically incompetent group. The 'bloke in the pub', though, is ignorant, bigoted and working class. By comparing MCC members to this figure Steel also undermines their social pretence – they may belong to an exclusive club, but they are really no better than the pub bore.

The final paragraph returns to the points made at the beginning. It sees the failure to play Sri Lanka as an excuse based on bigotry and ignorance and implies that cricket is run by authorities who are out of touch with the real world.

Sport is inextricably linked to the politics of a nation and to its national identity, although this is not usually officially admitted. In apartheid South Africa the white regime attempted to seek legitimacy through sporting contacts with the outside world. On gaining power, Nelson Mandela made a point of openly supporting his country's cricket and rugby teams, this time to give impetus to a sense of change, of a new beginning. US presidential candidates appear at ball games as part of their electioneering, and British political leaders increasingly identify themselves with sports teams, local and national; to be a sports fan is to be part of the nation, one of us. Sport can be used to support a national identity which may be rooted in a constructed stereotype, but one which politicians are keen to endorse. Language plays a key role in this process.

Extension

A vast range of sporting events offer you the chance to explore the way language contributes to a sense of national identity. The annual 5 Nations Rugby Union Tournament, for instance, will provide interesting data on the Englishman, the Scotsman, the Welshman and the Irishman, as well as the Frenchman.

To see how nations use sport to create a sense of their own identity, it would be interesting to collect data on American sports, especially baseball and American football. Because these games are essentially

American, and played only rarely elsewhere, the coverage will allow you to see how Americans use their national sports to create a picture of their own national identity. You could, for example, look for references to drama, elation, romance and dreams, qualities which are often found in film portrayals of these American sports.

Unit four

Sporting codes

The word **code** is used by linguists to refer to a language variety in which grammar and vocabulary are particular to a specific group. These codes can be a product of region, social background, age, ethnicity, and a common interest or activity. All occupations, to varying degrees, have a code that relates to their particular field of activity. The more specialised the occupation, the more technical language there is likely to be; the world of advanced computing for instance has many items of vocabulary which are beyond the understanding of most people, even those who regularly use computers. Those occupations which have long traditions are likely to go beyond the use of distinctive lexical items; religion, the law, medicine and education all have linguistic rituals which involve not only vocabulary but also grammar and types of discourse.

The use of such occupational codes produces a number of different attitudes. Those who use the code claim that it helps precision and is economical – a few words, sometimes themselves **initialisms** or **acronyms**, sufficing when many more would otherwise be needed. Most students will be familiar with at least some of the initialisms and acronyms in the field of education: GCSE, GNVQ, KS4, SCAA, etc. Indeed, the currency of such acronyms becomes so common that few stop to think that GCSE actually stands for the General Certificate of Secondary Education. Certainly GCSE is used without explanation in all the media and throughout schools and colleges.

Another justification of occupational codes is that like regional and social dialects, they can provide solidarity, make people feel part of a group. For some, though, occupational codes can be a source of annoyance. These are usually outsiders, people who are not part of the privileged group that has knowledge of and access to the code. They claim that occupational code is impossible to understand, that it is exclusive, keeping outsiders in their place. Very few of us can have direct access to the legal system, for instance, however trivial a case may be. We have to seek the help of lawyers, not so much to understand the law but to cope with the language and the rituals which surround its application.

Campaigns such as the Plain English Campaign have argued that government bodies, and other institutions, should be clear in their meaning and avoid the obscurity that can come with occupational code. The legal profession, not surprisingly, argues that legal English is not deliberately obscure, but that it is necessarily precise to ensure that the law is applied with absolute clarity. So the same code is perceived by its users to be an example of clarity, by those who do not use it as an obstacle to understanding.

David Crystal, in his *Encyclopedia of the English Language* (1995) highlights these contrasting views when he defines the word **jargon** in his glossary. Jargon, originally meaning 'the twittering of birds', is a word often used to describe, usually critically, the vocabulary of occupational code. Crystal gives two meanings which highlight the different attitudes held towards specialist language: '1. The technical language of a special field' and '2. The obscure use of specialised language'. For those who use the specialised language it is a sign of technical expertise, for those who do not it is obscure and confusing.

Every sport, whether it is played professionally as an occupation, or whether it is simply followed by amateur enthusiasts has its own specialised code. Where the sports are relatively minor and followed largely by those who actually take part, this use of codes causes no controversy. Indeed novices at the sport are likely to make great efforts to acquire the code as soon as possible, so that they can be part of the group.

Activity

The sport of canoeing has little public exposure. You are unlikely to know many of the actual terms, unless you are a canoeist, but you can probably predict what general categories these terms can be placed into. Make a list of these categories and add any terms which you may have heard of.

Commentary

The first category you may have predicted would be terms for types of craft and paddles. So there are the terms 'canoe' and 'kayak', the difference being that a canoe is propelled by a single-bladed paddle, a kayak by a double-bladed one. A second category contains terms for specialist clothing worn by the canoeist. 'Pogies' are large gloves, 'spraydecks' are skirts worn round the waist and fitted over the canoe to stop water getting in. A third category involves highly specific terms for water features, such as 'stopper', 'hole', 'eddy', 'drop', 'chute', 'rapid', 'cushion wave', 'towback', etc. The successful canoeist needs to know the precise geography of the course to be covered and specialist terms are needed to identify the different features. Naming them helps in their negotiation. Another category involves terms for manoeuvres such as 'pop-out', 'tail squirt', 'ferry glide', 'shudder rudder', etc.

You were probably able to predict these categories, because even if you know little about the sport it is likely that canoeists will require technical terms for their equipment, for the terrain they use and for their methods of making progress. What you would not know were the terms themselves, especially the highly specialised ones. As a newcomer to the sport you would soon acquire these terms, because they would be used in your instruction and would form part of the way you mentally processed the necessary skills. At the same time you would use them with fellow canoeists to show that you were just that, a fellow canoeist. If, however, you used them with friends who had no knowledge of or interest in the sport, you would soon be seen as a bore. With friends you would be much more likely to use vague, more general terms.

However, when sports are more popular, with a large public following, criticisms of obscurity and the unnecessary use of code often occur. Ken Jones, a leading sportswriter, complained in the *Independent* about footballers and football writers who:

> ... never fail to convey the impression that football is an art so involved and technical as to be removed from ordinary knowledge and understanding. In their eagerness to pose as experts they fill the air with fashionable theories and jargon, ignoring an unassailable truth, which is that sport is best served by uncomplicated conclusions. . . . In the language of television commentators, to have a poor defence is to be weak at the back, and when every player gives of his best a team is 'totally committed'. Corners and free-kicks have long since become dead-ball situations, and forwards who run intelligently into space are said to be probing the gullies.

49

Activity

Discuss, in pairs or groups if possible, the following:

1   Jones says that there is an 'unassailable truth' about the way sport is reported. What is this 'truth', and do you agree with his view?
2   Why do you think football experts use language which Jones calls 'involved and technical'?

Commentary

The 'unassailable truth' that sport is 'best served' by uncomplicated language goes against the way language is used in other fields of expertise. One way the experts can show their expertise is by using occupational code; if they displayed ordinary knowledge, they would be seen as ordinary and not worth listening to. Jones, though, accuses the experts of posing. His view seems in part to stem from the idea that sport is somehow outside the everyday world, occupying a special place in our society; that the language which surrounds it should have a simplicity not found in other forms of social discourse.

Language use is constantly changing, changes which can involve vocabulary, grammar and pronunciation. Such changes are often resisted at first and seen as a sign of falling standards – even sometimes of falling moral standards. What often offends those who complain about sporting code is that new additions are constantly made to it. Jones gives as a particular example to support his case the way 'corners and free-kicks have long since become dead-ball situations, and forwards who run intelligently into space are said to be probing the gullies'. Yet in his example Jones uses specialist terms that could just as easily be called code: 'forwards who run intelligently into space', for example. In this case, though, the phrase has been in use long enough for it to be generally accepted. It was stated earlier that specialist code can be economical in its use of words; here the phrase 'totally committed' says in two words what would otherwise take more and is thus very useful to a commentator who is having to speak as the action unfolds.

Occupational code, especially in the fast-developing world of sport, is as subject to change as any other sort of language, and when the sport has major coverage in the media such change often leads to ridicule and condemnation.

Collect some examples of code that is used by writers and/or commentators for a sport of your choice. Try to list these examples under the following headings and then compare your findings with other members of your class or group.

1   Well-established or traditional terms for (a) positions on the field, (b) specialist roles, (c) specialist equipment and (d) types of physical contact.
2   Words and phrases which you think may be recent additions to the sport's terminology.

The following are examples of well-established sporting terms, all used here as nouns. Name the sport or sports which use them and then, using a dictionary which includes etymological references where necessary, see if you can research the origin of the term.

pole position   silly mid on
southpaw   kiss
heat   midfielder
seed   stroke
yellow jersey   a short head
bogey   tramlines

Many of the terms in sporting codes serve the purpose of economy of language, allowing a few words to replace many. An example of this is the word 'midfielder' from football. It identifies certain sorts of players by using the approximate area of the pitch in which they operate. Because the term, first used in the 1960s, did not clearly differentiate between types of midfielder, further qualification has since been added; players are now usually called an 'attacking or defensive midfielder'. A midfielder who is good enough to do all jobs, and to control the game is called a 'midfield general', thus again linking sport with war. The rowing term 'stroke' serves a similar function, referring to the position held in the boat by the rower who determines the stroke rate of the whole crew.

51

'Stroke' also refers to hitting the ball in tennis and similar games.

The use of **synecdoche**, part for whole, is shown in the cycling term 'yellow jersey'. The race leader traditionally wears a yellow jersey, so this term is used to describe the leader and changes in the race leadership. As with all code, the phrase 'the yellow jersey changed hands today' only makes sense if you understand the reference, if you are interested enough in cycling to share the code.

A large amount of sporting code is metaphorical in origin; sometimes the source of the metaphor is clear, at other times the original source of the metaphor may not at first be apparent. The snooker term 'kiss' refers to a slight collision between two balls, and the tennis term 'tramlines' refers to the two parallel lines which are used in doubles matches. A 'short head' is a small winning margin in horse racing. The cricket term 'silly mid on' refers to a position so close to the bat, that the fielder is in some danger, he is silly to be so close.

Other examples of sporting code show the complex changes that can occur in meaning and use over time. 'Pole position', which is the leading position on the starting grid of a motor race, comes originally from horse racing in the USA. The 'pole lane' was the name given to the inside lane on a race course. 'Pole position' refers to one of a number of markers placed at intervals of one-sixteenth of a mile along the side of a racecourse. Presumably this idea of a marker on a track has been used metaphorically to describe the best position. 'Southpaw' is an American term for a sportsplayer who is left-handed. It is said to originate from a Chicago journalist who was describing a baseball match; the baseball park faced west, so a left-hander would have that hand facing south. In Britain the term is only used for left-handers in boxing, however.

The word 'bogey' refers to the score when a golf hole is played in one shot over par, par being the standard score expected on that hole. This word has a detailed history. 'Bogey' comes originally from the idea of playing an imaginary opponent, a bogey man, who would notionally make the standard score. Like the game of golf itself, this word comes from Scotland. 'Bogey' therefore meant the standard score until a new type of golf ball was introduced in 1898. This ball could be hit further, so standard scores were reduced by one shot. At the same time the game had spread to the USA and it was the the American usage 'par' which was adopted for the standard notional score. This means that the word 'bogey' stood still and remained where it was, in the process changing its meaning. Instead of the standard score it became one shot over standard, and in the process showed the huge influence of American English (see Bryson, 1994).

The tennis term 'seed' is also American in origin, coming from the idea that the best results are achieved by planting seeds a certain distance apart. Keeping the best players apart is the underlying principle behind the sporting use of seeding.

One suggested origin of the word 'heat' is that it was originally used in horse racing to describe a run given to a horse before a big race, a sort of warm-up. The word's meaning has then shifted slightly as it has been transferred to athletics, meaning not a warm-up but a preliminary race which leads to a final.

The level playing field

Sporting code shows the way language evolves and changes. It also shows how many terms are metaphorical in origin, even if the source of such metaphors has sometimes become obscured. The relationship between sport and metaphor is a two-way one, however; not only are many sporting terms metaphorical in origin, drawing on other fields of activity for their semantic connection, but sport increasingly acts as a source of metaphors too.

Recent work on semantics in English has looked at the place of metaphor in everyday speech (for example, Lakoff and Johnson, 1980). Metaphor is deeply embedded in the way we construct the world around us, and the way that world is constructed for us by others. One example involves the metaphorical idea that our bodies are containers, with our emotions as substances within them: 'he boiled over with anger', 'she simmered with rage', 'he blew his top' (see Goddard, 1996).

Another example involves the metaphorical idea that life is ruled by chance, that it is a gamble. Hence we 'take a chance', 'hazard a guess', 'play our cards right', 'play our cards close to our chest', 'have the luck of the draw', 'play for high stakes', etc. This suggests a view of our lives where we are not certain of control, where we can shift the blame for failure onto external forces. Many sportsplayers talk in terms of chance and luck as being central to their success or failure.

Sport, then, also provides the source of many metaphors used in everyday life. This is only to be expected when sport plays such a major role in the media and in our lives generally. The way these metaphors are used, however, also tells us something about sport's role in our mental picture of the society we inhabit.

Football for instance gives us a number of metaphors that are used by politicians: 'moving the goalposts', which means changing the conditions that apply to something, perhaps coming from the idea of children playing football and using coats as goals which can be easily moved; 'a level playing field', which means conditions are fair for all, there is no slope to favour one side or the other. These two metaphors are rooted in the idea that sport is somehow fair and that politics should be too, if only the opposition stopped bending the rules. 'Scoring an own goal' is often used to describe politicians who have harmed their own cause by making a mistake; while 'it's a long shot' means a try at something which is unlikely to succeed, but which just might, like the distant shot on goal in football.

Activity

Working in pairs or groups if possible, compile a list of metaphors in everyday use which come from the following sports: cricket/baseball, golf, tennis, athletics.

You may then, if you wish, look at other sports too.

Commentary

As was seen in Unit 1, the connotations which relate to the game of cricket have created a mythical picture of the game. Not surprisingly, everyday metaphors tend to reinforce this view. 'It's not cricket' refers to unfair practice of any sort. If you give little away you 'play with a straight bat'; if things are difficult you are 'batting on a sticky wicket' and will perhaps 'settle for a draw'. On his appointment to a senior position in the BBC recently, a director said 'I want to play myself in slowly', comparing a high-profile job to an innings in cricket.

The director of OFWAT, a watchdog over the privatised water companies in Britain, used two sporting metaphors when challenged about the huge wastage of water caused by broken pipes. He said: 'Water companies have taken their eye off the ball and it's my job to get them back on track', so combining a cricketing term with one from some form of racing. In saying that the companies had 'taken their eye off the ball', though, he used an expression which seems to lessen the failings of the companies – their offence becomes a minor one, a sporting error rather than a serious economic and political issue. Likewise his view of his job, that it is 'to get them back on track', lacks the punitive edge that should be expected of someone appointed to safeguard the public interest.

If cricket provides a number of common metaphors for English speakers, so baseball does the same for Americans. Although the two games have common roots, they have very different cultural associations; the American game is seen as a more aggressive, more competitive sport. (There has to be a winner in baseball, draws are not allowed.) Something different is 'a whole new ball game'; economists talk of 'a ball-park figure'; to fail is to be 'back at first base'. 'To play ball' is to co-operate (an English equivalent is the more general 'to play the game'). The idea of a 'raincheck', a ticket which allows you back into a baseball game once it has stopped raining, is now used by British supermarkets to promise a special offer when supplies are replenished. The word 'fan' originated from baseball, as a short form of 'fanatic'.

Among others you may have listed, from golf come 'par for the course', 'bunkered'; from tennis come 'game, set and match', 'a subtle lob', 'hit out of court'; from athletics 'from the word go', 'running order', 'jump the gun', 'false start'.

Because sport has such a central place in our society, it is not surprising that it gives so many metaphors to our everyday language. These metaphors also help to reflect and reinforce a social and economic system that is based on competition, on winners and losers. Sport is legitimised competition, apparently played fairly to a set of rules – although the rules are often bent if not actually broken in sport, just as they are in other activities. No wonder then that sporting metaphors are particularly popular with politicians. Indeed, as was noted in Unit 3, sport is important to leading political figures in many countries; they are seen at sporting events, and many increasingly use sporting metaphors to sell their policies.

The word 'sport' and associated words have a number of uses and meanings. A 'good sport' can be someone who plays by the rules and is fair, or someone who bends the rules and likes a good time. It can also refer to someone who is happy to have a joke made at their expense, or someone who plays that joke. A 'sportsman' can be someone who is good at sport but also someone who can take defeat gracefully. 'Sportswoman', on the other hand, tends to be used only for women who make sport a career. 'Good sportsmanship' can be used to describe the tactics of victory or the good grace of defeat. A 'sports' car is racy, fast, and a similar meaning is implied when someone is said to be 'sporty' in behaviour or appearance. A 'sporting' act can be a generous act as well as an athletic one.

A number of semantic connotations, some of them contradictory, surround the family of words based on 'sport' – these include 'athleticism', 'fairness', 'daring', 'joking', 'good manners', 'success', 'failure'. This range is what might be expected when we consider that sport operates within society, not outside it, even though it has suited

55

many to project the view that sport is somehow outside the social and political mainstream. Analysis of some of the ways in which language is used to construct an idea of sport, and how the language of sport is used to construct a view of society, shows how interwoven they really are.

Extension

All sports provide examples of their own codes. Because major sports are usually well documented, an interesting piece of research would be to collect data on a 'minority' sport, similar to canoeing, mentioned in this unit. You could then examine the origins of the terms and look at their use of metaphor.

Sportstalk I

People who talk about sport are much better known than those who write about it. This is not surprising when you consider that major sporting events are watched on television by huge audiences. Satellite broadcasting means that there are whole channels given over entirely to sport, and with so much time to fill, there is now a massive coverage of a whole range of sport. Radio too is drawing increasingly high audiences as stations become more specialised - focusing on one area of output, such as sport or different kinds of music.

Commentators, because of the large audiences, often become closely associated with the sport they specialise in. When first radio and then television started to cover live sport, there were very few commentators; whatever the sport, one of a handful of commentators would cover the event. Nowadays, with sport an increasingly important player in the search for audiences, there is massive coverage, and each sport has its own specialist commentators.

There are two reasons for this. One is that the commentators have specialist knowledge of the game, its tactics and its terminology. The other is that very different linguistic skills are required to talk about the various sports. Compare golf on television with horse racing, for instance. A major golf tournament lasts four days, a horse race a few minutes. A horse race has a continuous flow of action, leading to a winner. Golf has a whole series of smaller contests, with each hole an event within an event. Identification of horses in a race is much more complex than naming a golfer. The camera stays fixed on the race's continuous action, whereas in golf it has time to wander off and survey the crowd, surroundings, and so on. All of this is reflected in the spoken language that is used.

Activity

This activity will introduce you to some issues about spoken sporting language and it will also show you some issues surrounding the collection of data – this will be particularly useful if you are thinking of doing some research work in this field.

Choose two sports which are going to be televised during the time you are working on this unit. Any two sports will do but if possible choose two sports which are very different in their pace and duration; possible 'fast' sports could be horse racing, motor racing, sprinting, skiing, rugby; possible 'slow' or 'long' games could be golf, snooker, cricket, marathon running. For each sport record some data from television. It helps at this stage if you record a whole event, or a good part of it, so that you have a reasonable amount of material to draw on.

Once you have recorded the data, sort through it and look for a few minutes which are going to give you some useful and typical material. The shorter events, like a horse race, will be relatively self-contained; on the longer event you might record three hours of cricket, but use a five-minute section when a wicket falls, or something controversial happens.

When you have selected your material, make a transcript of each piece. This can take time, because eventually you will need to record not only the language but also the pictures which accompany it. Some conventions of transcription are included in Unit 6, if you wish to use them, but at this stage the most important things for you to do are to record the spoken language accurately, to take note of timings and pauses, and to mark points at which volume and/or stress are especially high.

When you have done all this, prepare answers to the following questions. First compare your responses for each of the two sports you covered; then, if you are a member of a class or group, compare your answers with those of others covering different sports.

Even if you do not have time to complete the written transcripts, you can watch some television sport and see if you can answer at least some of the questions.

1   What variations of speed of talking did you find?
2   What variations of volume and stress did you find?

3 What specialist/technical words and phrases did you find which relate to a specific sport?
4 To what extent was the language used influenced by the pictures on the screen?
5 Did the commentators have any ways of speaking which followed certain patterns, such as use of certain words, grammatical structures?
6 How did the commentators, if there was more than one, interact?
7 How did the commentators address you, the audience? How did they try to interest you, and what picture of their sport did they try to present?

Each of these questions asks you to investigate an important feature of sports commentary. You could use these as a starting point for a longer piece of research.

Some commentators become so linked with their sport that their commentaries and personalities are seen as somehow representative of the sport itself. A few are accorded great status, especially those linked to sports such as golf and cricket which like to think they have a strong moral and social ethos. Such commentators are often given, or indeed give themselves, a guardianship of the values that the games are said to hold dear.

Cricket, in particular, has had commentators who have become as important as the players. John Arlott received a standing ovation from the crowd when he finished his last radio test-match commentary (they were listening to him while watching the game!). John Major when prime minister said that 'Summers will never be the same again' on the death of another radio commentator, Brian Johnston.

Richie Benaud, the television commentator, is thought by many to be one of the best commentators; he was described by the television critic Andrew Baker as 'the greatest cricket commentator of the age: knowledgeable, amusing and – most priceless gift of all – silent when there is nothing to say'.

Baker's comments show we do, as an audience, pass judgement on commentators, and assess their performance. You will notice that qualities he looks for are knowledge of the game, humour, and the ability, in a television commentator, to let the pictures speak for themselves. (The requirements of a radio commentator, who has to paint word pictures, are very different, as you will see in the next unit.)

Cricket may have more famous commentators than most games because of the relatively slow nature of the game, and because of the cultural associations we make with the game (see Unit 1). On the other hand motor racing's most famous commentator Murray Walker is best known for the noise and screeching of his commentary – almost as though he is shouting above the din of the cars, which indeed he sometimes is. The commentary, then, is shaped by the nature of the game but at the same time helps to define that game for the viewing public – it is a two-way process.

Some commentators are disliked and seen as irritating, though; for various reasons their vocal style does not appeal to audiences. Sometimes it is because of tone of voice, or accent, sometimes because of the emotional pitch at which they operate.

Popularisers of sport also tend to fall foul of critics. When Rugby League was a minority sport it was screened regularly on television, presumably because it was cheap. The commentator who became known as the 'voice of rugby league' was Eddie Waring, a sort of cheeky northern chappy. Although popular in parts of the country where the game was not played, he was hated and reviled by those northeners who supported it. They interpreted his commentary, including his strong northern accent, as a sort of music-hall turn, cheapening their game and holding up their culture to mockery.

Others felt that Brian Johnston, who certainly broadened the appeal of cricket on the radio by his references to cream cakes and his general social warmth, did so at the expense of taking the game seriously. Many of those who were attracted to his commentary would not actually go to see a match; in other words, claimed his critics, he was creating a false picture and his own cult of personality. John Major's suggestion that Johnston epitomised the English summer only helped to confirm the suspicions of some.

When television coverage of sport was restricted to terrestrial stations, and so relatively infrequent, individual commentators became strongly linked to sports or sporting events. Dan Maskell was 'the voice of tennis', Peter Alliss the 'voice of golf', Peter O'Sullivan's the voice most associated with horse racing. Even football, the most covered sport in Britain, has had relatively few commentators; the BBC, for instance, kept the same two main commentators through most of the 1970s, 1980s and 1990s.

Activity

Devising and using questionnaires can provide useful information on attitudes to language, which are often strongly held. The more people you ask, the more reliable are the conclusions that can be drawn.

Devise a short questionnaire which aims to find out: (1) which commentators are identified with which sports; (2) whether people can identify any particular features of that commentator's style of presentation; (3) whether people have any particular likes or dislikes among the commentators.

Spot the balls up

The ambivalent relationship between audiences and commentators, some loved, some hated, and many a bit of both, gained a wider currency when the satirical magazine *Private Eye* started a column called Colemanballs. It was named after the commentator David Coleman and was a collection of linguistic 'cock-ups' made by commentators and sent in by readers.

It still continues today and is often quoted in mockery at commentators, nearly all of whom appear somewhere in the various editions. In one sense though they are easy targets; commentary is an instant response to something happening at the time, and all unplanned talk lacks the elegant coherence, and sometimes strict sense, that can be achieved when writing. When the athletics commentator John Rawlins, concentrating on the performance of the English athlete Sally Gunnell, said on radio 'She's behind the woman in front of her' it did not at the time of the race seem as stupid a comment as it does here in print, when the reader has time to contemplate the logic of the statement.

The fact that most listeners do not even spot the 'mistakes' suggests rather more about the nature of what commentary actually is – unscripted, spontaneous talk, aiming to capture the on-going excitement of the event. Indeed in the early years of sports commentary the phrase 'running commentary' was used. It was a useful reminder, in an age when most broadcast talk was scripted, that the commentary 'ran on' spontaneously.

Below is a list of so-called mistakes attributed to the football commentator John Motson.

We're back to 1-1.

The World Cup – truly an international event.

Nearly all the Brazilian supporters are wearing yellow shirts. It's a fabulous kaleidoscope of colour.

Oh, that's good running on the run.

It's a football stadium in the truest sense of the word.

England under siege now, perhaps for the first time in a length of time.

Platt – singularly in two minds.

Peter Reid is hobbling and I've got a feeling that will slow him down.

The game is balanced in Arsenal's favour.

When given a second thought, these are amusing, even surreal in their effect. It is unlikely, though, that many viewers would have noticed anything wrong with 'it's back to 1-1' in the context of a live game, a goal having just been scored, and the continuous flow of talk that would have followed. The overall sense of the phrase – the teams are level – would have been communicated, rather than the illogicality which can only really be worked out when the words are seen in print.

Activity

Using the examples from John Motson above (and then, if you wish, finding others of your own), see how many of the speakers' intended meanings you can work out.

It is important that students of language take an objective view of sports commentary and of the commentators, even if others do not, and that you recognise how speaking and writing involve very different skills. Because talk is spontaneous, and sports talk is even more complex, because it has to report simultaneously what is seen with the eye, there is always an element of chance in the process. One of the most famous and often repeated pieces of commentary comes from the 1966 World Cup final. As Geoff Hurst advanced on the German goal, the BBC commentator Kenneth Wolstenholme said, 'Some people are on the pitch. They think it's all over. It is now.' Meanwhile on ITV Hugh Johns was saying, 'Geoff Hurst goes forward. He might make it three. He has, he has. And that's it, that's it.' The substance of the two comments is very similar, but the first one is often idiomatically repeated in many different contexts and has even provided the name of a television sports quiz show, whereas the second is forgotten.

Just as features of language such as pronunciation, meaning, grammar, are constantly changing, so is the way language is put to specific occupational use. The sports commentators of today use language differently from those of the past. There are various reasons for this. Their pronunciation is less likely to be the Received Pronunciation that was standard in the early days of broadcasting – this is true in many other areas of broadcasting too, reflecting changing attitudes to regional speech. The range of vocabulary is different too, reflecting developments in sports science as an academic subject, covering such areas as sports psychology, sports physiology and sports technology.

Increasingly specialised vocabulary not only reflects scientific advances, it is also a reflection of sport's changing social role. As more time is spent on the coverage of sport, and so on the watching of it, and more money surrounds professional sport, so sports commentators need to acquire a wider linguistic repertoire. There are a number of reasons for this: specialist language gives a sport status, uniqueness; this uniqueness adds to the sport's commercial value; specialised language can be impressive, giving weight and substance to a sport; it can act as a bond, a mutual link between those who play, those who commentate and to an extent those who watch.

Other changes in the language of commentators are the result of increasing sophistication in the technology of broadcasting sport, especially on television. Satellite links worldwide, multiple cameras, slow motion replays, all require spoken language to accompany them. On radio there have been fewer obvious technical advances, although changes in commentary technique still occur.

This happens in particular with sports whose action tends to be very fast. Early commentators tried to describe all that happened, and often became very good at talking fast. The following is an extract from a tennis commentary on a match between Laver and Milligan in the early 1960s. The rally described lasted 13 seconds, and in that time the commentator used 74 words. This means that on average, during the action, he was speaking at 342 words per minute.

> Game point to Laver as Milligan serves down the centre backhand return down the line Milligan at full stretch but he is out of court Laver crosses him Milligan gets it through magnificently but he's out of court again he gets it once again Laver a half volley Milligan's there to take it and put it down the line Laver once again and Laver's beaten him with a backhand volley down the line.

Although commentary like this was very skilful, it went ahead of the audience's ability to see events in their mind's eye. Even seeing it written down it becomes very difficult to draw a diagram of what happened; hear it and it becomes impossible. On television a point such as this would have no comment until it was over, but radio cannot have long silences; as a medium it requires almost constant talk. The radio commentators, therefore, have had to develop a different technique, one which gives a sense of the action, but which can at least in part help the audience to visualise what is happening.The following is a transcript of a point played in a match between Henman and Gustaffson at Wimbledon in 1996. It lasts 15 seconds and contains 41 words. Henman is a British player, playing in front of a home crowd.

> [Sound of ball being served by Gustaffson at the beginning of the point] and a forehand reply of the first point of the tie break and here comes Henman with a forehand and Gustaffson goes cross court and Henman's in behind his forehand Henman's there for a volley into the empty court (.) first point to Henman.

Activity

Both rallies last roughly the same amount of time, yet the 1996 commentary uses significantly fewer words. If you study the transcripts carefully, you can work out that there are ten shots in the 1960 rally and eight in the 1996 rally. Make a list of the descriptions of each shot, leaving a blank line where a shot has not been described. Then make notes on the following questions:

1   What strategies does the 1996 commentator use in order to say fewer words? Look, for example, at the naming of players and the use of adverbial words and phrases.
2   What methods does each commentator use to connect the various phrases so that there is a sense of continuing action?
3   Compare the way each commentator brings the point to a close.

What does it feel like?

So far in this unit the word 'commentator' has been used to cover all those who talk about sport on television or radio. The broadcast big match, though, contains a number of different roles, each with its own distinctive linguistic features, features governed in turn by the nature of the medium, whether it be radio or television. In addition to the running commentary there is the role of the commentator's expert assistant;

there are the studio experts who contribute before, in the middle and at the end of the match; there are the post-event interviews. The more coverage that is given to sport, the more air time to fill, then more people are needed to talk about the sport from as many angles as possible. The whole package gives an entertainment which goes well beyond the game itself: a 90-minute football match on satellite television will be contained within three and a half hours of viewing, including a large number of advertisements. It is the adverts, it must be remembered, which make the television company's profit, and it is the sport which encourages the audience to watch the adverts.

One of the most common pieces of sports coverage is the post-event interview. In many sports players and officials are obliged by contract to give interviews after an event and it is increasingly common for players to be interviewed even while they are still on the pitch. These interviews often follow a set formula – what does it feel like? how did you see the winning goal? These questions often lead to very bland replies, but the fact that the action can be prolonged, and the stars seen in close-up, is often justification enough.

Football team managers are some of the most frequently interviewed, being asked to account for the performance of their team. One notable feature of these interviews is that they seem to involve very few questions; after a fairly general question has been asked, the managers take their cue to speak at length on a range of topics. Indeed the question asked is often omitted from the interview if it is recorded, and the managers are seen talking without interruption. A leading football manager has said, 'Of all the things expected of me, I find speaking to the media immediately after matches the most difficult'. One way of coping with this pressure can be to continue talking; if they are talking, they cannot be asked further, more probing questions.

The following two transcripts are interviews with leading managers in 1996. The first is with the manager of the England football team, Terry Venables. England had just beaten Hungary 3-0. The second is with the Manchester United manager Alex Ferguson after his team had won the 1996 cup final and so won the double (i.e. league and cup) for the second year running. No question preceded this interview when it was broadcast. Pauses are marked in brackets. (.) means less than one second, (1) means the number of seconds.

Activity

Read the two interviews and give a paraphrase of what each manager says. Then look at the way each manager ensures that he is not interrupted by further questions. What do you notice about each manager's use of pronouns?

(a) *Question*: What particularly pleased you about your performance today?

Venables: Well I wasn't very happy at all the first (.) twenty four twenty five minutes (1) er we was a bit we was a bit static (1) and er we couldn't find the space to hit the front men at all but that was our fault rather than the opposition (.) blocking the way that was (.) more down to us that's what disappointed me (.) erm (.) and we got it got word on to to change it and do actually what we'd been doing (.) erm (1) and then it opened up (.) we started get space the front players got more room (.) erm if you realise in the first half like (.) people like Teddy was having to well come well deep cause they couldn't find any space (.) so that really (.) disappointed me there (1) but we we moved the wingers up and wide and the wider midfield players a bit wider so there was lots of space for the front players score their goal (.) and that give us a even more of a boost and didn't look back from there really

(b) *Ferguson*: At the end of the day (4) there are times when you say to yourself well the result's important (1) I think it's important in this respect for us that (2) we've we've gone to (.) a tremendous (.) pinnacle (.) this year with the young with so many young players without the experience that we've had in the past (2) and the result was very important for our supporters (.) it's (1) it's a landmark it's the first team to do a double double it's fantastic for the players and supporters (1) so at the end of the day (1) there has (.) I have to be (1) sort of erm (.) clinical in (.) my assessment of the situation (.) the result brilliant (1) but the sort of performance I could put in the back of my head because I know we can play better

Commentary

Neither manager says very much in terms of content. Venables says that the team played better once the wing players moved forward – although this does not directly answer the question he was asked. Ferguson says he was delighted with the victory, although the team could have played better. It is an unwritten rule that managers do not criticise players in public. In these interviews only one player is actually named, and he is referred to by his first name.

Political interviewees are often given a difficult time by interviewers, who will interrupt, fire lots of questions, refer to past statements, etc. Managers are not put under the same pressure — neither interviewer speaks once the answer has begun. The managers, though, do seem to have strategies in making sure that they give a speech of their choosing rather than an interview. Venables speaks very fast and links his utterances with a string of **connectives**: 'and', 'so', 'but'. Sometimes his **filler** 'erm' make sure that he cannot be interrupted.

Ferguson is much more hesitant, with false starts and long pauses; the first, of four seconds, comes when he has said nothing beyond the **phatic** 'at the end of the day'. He turns this hesitation to his advantage, though, by never obviously being near to the completion of a semantic unit; 'so at the end of the day (1) there has (.) I have to be (1) sort of erm (.) clinical (.)' is such a loosely connected collection of words and phrases that it makes interruption highly unlikely.

Pronouns are always an interesting feature of managers' interviews. The manager is both part of the team, yet distant from it; he is responsible for the team's result but he has not actually played in the game. Both managers use 'we'/'us' to identify the collective effort, but sometimes use 'I'/'me', especially when they are criticising their teams, either explicitly or implicitly. The first person pronoun 'I'/'me' allows some distance between the manager and his players.

Footballers and football managers in particular are often singled out for public ridicule for the way they speak in interviews. There is sometimes an element of elitism in this criticism, coming as it does from professional writers and talkers; footballers and managers are not trained to talk publicly to the media, which is especially difficult immediately after a game. At first sight Venables displays many of the linguistic features that have been derided; he uses a large amount of occupational dialect, language that is specific to the tactics of football, and also some low-prestige regional dialect. Ferguson uses more metaphorical language but seems to struggle to complete the metaphors — he does not appear to be very clinical in his assessment.

It can be argued, though, that these two managers have in fact devised coping strategies which keep the interviewers at a distance. They have to provide words for the media output, yet they are severely limited as to what they can actually say — to criticise players would make their own job more difficult, to criticise referees would lead to punishment by the authorities. In saying very little, they achieve their objective, and so to that extent their talk is rather more sophisticated than may at first appear. It also helped, in their cases, that they had won their matches.

Extension

Collect some post-match interviews with sports players, coaches and managers, either in transcript form or on tape. Delete the questions asked and play the answers to various members of your group. Their task is (1) to work out as soon as possible whether the person has been a winner or a loser and (2) work out what questions were asked.

When you have done this, and discussed your findings with the group, you will have gained some useful insights into some of the linguistic features of such interviews. Further research could involve a detailed look at various examples of post-match interviews within one sport, or comparing how leading figures in different sports talk in post-match interviews.

Sportstalk II

This unit will take a closer look at the language of commentary, comparing (1) the way two television channels covered the same match and (2) how radio commentary, also of the same match, has its own distinct linguistic features. The data will all relate to the match between England and Germany in the semi-finals of the Euro 96 tournament.

Many students choose to do research projects on the language of commentary and one of the first things they notice is how much language is generated by a single event – spoken accounts use many more words than written accounts. It is important, therefore, when tackling research in this area, to select a small, but significant segment of commentary and to look at it in detail.

In the England *v.* Germany match, England scored a goal after only 2 minutes of play. The data used in this unit will refer to the 80 seconds leading up to the goal, and the further 60 seconds following it. This amount of time will provide ample evidence for some linguistic analysis, although it will not, of course, reflect all the noteworthy features of commentary shown during the whole match.

When transcribing talk it is important to provide a full and clear key to the method you have used. There are no hard and fast rules to follow, provided you make it absolutely clear how you have proceeded. In the transcripts below the following conventions have been used.

1 Most punctuation, which is a feature of writing rather than speech, has been omitted, although capital letters have been used at the start of a turn and for the large number of proper nouns. Apostrophes have been used for short forms, i.e. 'there's', etc.

2 Silences are marked by a bracket ( ) with (.) meaning a pause of less than one second. Longer pauses have the number of seconds recorded, i.e. (3).

3 Particularly loud speech has been written in BLOCK CAPITALS.

4 Where words have been particularly stressed, they are underlined.

5 Where a sound is drawn out, or elongated, :: has been used.

6 C stands for the commentator, ES for the expert summariser.

There has been no attempt to mark intonation, or to depict regional varieties of speech.

Activity

For each transcript, research the following questions. Where possible try to compare the differences between the two transcripts.

1 What examples of specialist football language are found in the commentaries?

2 What words are used to describe the two countries, England and Germany, and their players? What differences do you notice and how do you account for them?

3 What are some of the most distinctive features of speech grammar seen here? You could focus on features such as verbs and verb tenses, use of prepositions, and ellipsis (the omission of words from a full utterance).

Television commentary 1 (T1)

C: It's Tony Adams (5) David Seaman says he doesn't really like the kit he has to play in tonight (1) can't exactly blame him (6) touch by Gascoigne this is McManaman (4) Shearer far post Sheringham even wider (1) for Pearce's cross (2) back in numbers the Germans (.) here's Paul Ince (.) that's a GOOD STRIKE (2) and it is Kopke (.) living up to his usual style (.) doesn't like to catch if he can possibly punch (.) took [action replay begins …] no chances with this one (2)

ES: It was a long way out (.) I suppose it was a good save but your timing's got to be perfect when you're punching those [... action replay ends] (.) he only had to tip it over you get the same end product (5)

C: McManaman is in front of the goalkeeper (4) and the referee's sorting out a little bit of pushing and shoving (1) Stefan Freund and McManaman (.) flick on AND SHEARER (2) WONDERFUL START (1) HIS FIFTH GOAL IN HIS FIFTH MATCH [camera on manager, etc.] THEY CAN'T QUITE BELIEVE IT ON THE BENCH (1) [camera on supporters] in the European championship (.) before coming here it took him twenty three to score five goals (.) when it's mattered <u>most</u> [action replays of goal] (1) Gascoigne's corner (.) flick on by Adams and <u>in</u> by Shearer

ES: Well it was straightforward stuff wasn't it (.) [action replay from different angle] to the near post (.) clears the first man Tony Adams between the two with the faintest of touches and where was the marker for Alan Shearer (1) we're not complaining the ball's in the back of the net [game back in progress] and a wonderful start (6)

C: England (1) taking the lead in two minutes and fifteen seconds (270 words)

Television commentary 2 (T2)

C: Big Tony Adams who seems to have grown even bigger with the England captain's armband (.) a really garish outfit (.) from our number one goalkeeper David Seaman (.) hit long by him (2) Freund knocking the ball forwards towards <u>Muller</u> who's in a <u>very</u> advanced position maybe they're going to play <u>Muller</u> more forward (.) in the meantime it's McManaman (1) Gascoigne had er made himself available Mc McManaman is obviously in the right frame of mind to take it on himself (.) an early cross in there from Stuart Pearce (.) banged away only as far as Paul Ince (.) Ince with the <u>volley</u> (.) fisted awa::y by Kopke (.) that was a <u>terrific shot</u> by Paul Ince (.)

ES: Well a very positive start from England [action replay starts ...] but this was a great shot it was never going to beat the keeper

71

but he takes no chances here but in the true German fashion of goalkeeping he punches it to safety (3) [... action replay ends]

C: Bright start for England (.) Gascoigne with the corner (.) Kopke who's just signed to play for Barcelona a two year contract with Bobby Robson out there (3) and referee Poul unhappy presumably with a little bit of argy bargy that's going on in the six yard area (.) it always happens (2) hit towards the near post a little flick <u>ON</u> IT'S A GOAL FOR <u>ENGLAND ALAN SHEARER SHEARER</u> HAS DONE IT AGAIN (.) HIS FIFTH <u>GOAL</u> IN <u>FIVE GAMES</u> (.) [camera on mangers, etc.] A <u>SMILE</u> FROM BRYAN ROBSON [camera on supporters] <u>DELIGHT</u> FROM THE ENGLISH FANS AND <u>THE PERFECT START</u> (1)

ES: [action replay begins] What a start this is we've been really deadly from set pieces but we really capitalised here (.) a flick on from Adams of all people to leave unmarked (.) Alan Shearer (1) that's his fifth goal (.) beautiful delivery from Gascoigne (.)

C: [game back in progress] A lovely flick on from Adams (.) a superb <u>swooping</u> header by Alan Shearer and England are <u>one</u> up (5) well we couldn't have hoped for anything better than that could we

(324 words)

Commentary

The use of specialist language is often criticised, the implication being that such terms are used deliberately to obscure meaning. This may well be the case in some circumstances, but not here – after all the purpose of commentary is to help the viewer, to clarify things, not to obscure them.

Specialist language appears in sports commentary for at least two reasons. First, it is a means of economy in language. 'Pearce's cross', says in two words what would otherwise need many more, i.e. 'Pearce kicks the ball high from the side of the pitch into the middle'. Second, it can add colour and drama to the account, often by using metaphorical description. For example, calling Ince's shot a 'strike' emphasises its aggressive force by likening it to a military onslaught.

The use of specialist language does depend, though, upon a shared understanding between commentator and viewer. This match had an audience in Britain of over 26 million, many of whom would have only a limited knowledge of the game and its code. The commentators, therefore, had to strike a balance between the useful economy and colour of footballing code and the danger of being too obscure.

The most obvious examples of specialist language in these two extracts involve descriptions of the geography of the pitch and descriptions of various types of contact with the ball. Some of these are listed below:

	Transcript 1	Transcript 2
Geography	a long way out	advanced position
	tip it over	move forward
	near post	6 yard area
	on the bench	near post
	ball's in the net	
Contact	cross	hit long
	flick on	knocking the ball forward
	faintest of touches	early cross
		banged away
		volley
		shot
		little flick on
		beautiful delivery.

It was noted above that sporting code can involve figurative language. The use of 'bench' to describe the substitutes, managers, trainers, etc. and 'the net' to represent the goal is technically called synecdoche – the representation of part for whole. In T2 the statement that 'Adams ... seems to have grown even bigger with the captain's armband' is another example of this – for 'armband' read 'the responsibilities that go with captaincy'. Using the one word to represent something bigger and more detailed can become a useful form of shorthand as well as lively and dramatic language. Many of the words for contact with the ball are metaphorical as in 'flick on' (this is literally something you do with your hand, which makes it a rather odd use for football), 'delivery' and a range of words like 'hit', 'knock', 'banged' which all suggest striking something. Other common words in this field, although not used here are 'hammer' and 'tap in'.

If one of the reasons for having commentary is to add colour to a game, then it is likely that in an international match commentators will show a certain amount of support for the home team – they can be confident that most of the viewers will agree. The word 'commentator', though, does suggest someone who is analytical, critical, neutral in stance. (The word 'commentary' has been used in exactly this way to describe the analytical sections in this book.) So commentators are not expected to be so obviously biased as some newspapers were before this particular match. In domestic games between teams from say Manchester and Liverpool they have to be even more careful in case they alienate the supporters of one side.

Transcript 1 takes a rather more neutral stance than Transcript 2. T1 sometimes refers to England players using first names and surnames, and does so once for a German player. T2 more consistently uses first names for English players and never does for German. In both transcripts there is the assumption that the goal is 'a wonderful start' or 'the perfect start', even though it was the opposite for the Germans of course. T2 uses more pronouns suggesting allegiance, with Seaman being 'our number one', while 'they're going to play'. Both commentaries emphasise the way Ince's shot is saved; T1 talks of Kopke's 'usual style', T2 that he saves 'in the true German fashion', the critical implication being that no English goalkeeper would have saved like that. Kopke, incidentally, went on to make the vital save in the penalty shoot-out.

As the coverage of sport has developed, larger numbers of people are employed to comment on a game; the main commentator is likely to be accompanied by an expert summariser, for instance, and this calls for sophisticated speaking skills. Normal conversation tends to have considerable overlap between speakers, even when they can make eye contact. The commentator and accomplice, though, sit side by side so are unable to use eye contact as a signal for who will speak when. Some pairs of commentators use physical signals for turn-taking, such as a dig in the ribs, whereas others use the rise and fall of intonation to organise their turns.

In these two transcripts, the action of the game in part determines when the experts will take a turn, and the pictures on the television often determine what is said, as commentators have to watch both the game and their monitor which shows them which pictures are being broadcast. Ince's shot is dramatic enough to warrant a replay, which gives the expert his chance to speak. Likewise with the goal — the main commentator describes the action first time, the expert then gives a review while watching the action replay on his monitor. An example of pictures determining speech is in T1; 'his fifth goal in his fifth match they can't quite believe it on the bench in the European championship'. Here the planned utterance, that it is his fifth goal in his fifth match in the European championship, has to be interrupted by the demands of the picture on screen. Although the resulting utterance seems strange when transcribed, it makes perfect sense on the television.

As can be seen in these two examples, the language of sports commentary is remarkably fluent, given that it is unscripted speech. There are few signs of hesitation noises, re-starts, words which do not make sense, unplanned pauses, etc. This is partly because the commentators are experienced practitioners, but also because they are working within certain linguistic conventions which help them.

One of the most obvious of these is the use of the present tense, at least by the main commentator – because the expert is reviewing the action, often with the aid of action replay, he is more likely to use the past tense. The use of the present tense takes several forms usually with some form of ellipsis involved. Ellipsis is the omission of words or phrases deemed not necessary. Sometimes the auxiliary use of 'to be' is omitted, as in 'Freund knocking the ball forwards', or 'banged away only as far as Ince'. The impersonal construction 'it is' (shortened to 'it's') is used frequently as in 'It's Tony Adams' and 'meantime it's McManaman'. which actually means that those players are in possession of the ball. At other points the verb itself is omitted as in 'Shearer far post' which means Shearer is standing by/running to the far post.

Also worth noting in commentary are passive constructions: 'an early cross in there from Stuart Pearce', 'fisted away by Kopke' (T2), 'touch by Gascoigne' (T1). Identification of players is an essential part of the commentator's job, and using a passive structure, putting the player's name last, gives the commentator a little extra time to identify the player. **Inversion** of word order can do the same job as in 'back in numbers the Germans' (T1).

The phrase 'far post' is one example of the use of words which give a sense of place and direction. The football pitch is a clearly defined area, with delineated areas, so spaces within it need to be signposted. This is frequently done by the use of **adverbial** words and phrases; some examples are 'forward', 'long', 'away', 'over', 'in front of', 'a long way out', 'in there', 'as far as', 'forward towards'. Transcript 2, which contains more detail and fewer pauses, uses considerably more of these adverbials than Transcript 1.

Deictics,which also give pointers to where things are, can be seen in 'that's a good strike', 'this one', 'in there', 'that was a terrific shot', 'this was a great shot'. 'That' tends to be used by the commentator as events happen, 'this' when the expert is reviewing events with an action replay. Deictics like 'this' and 'that' are always likely to be used in television commentaries because the commentator is reflecting in language what the viewer can see on the screen.

Pauses, especially micropauses, often replace connectives as in 'Ince with the volley (.) pushed away by Kopke'. Longer pauses, especially in T1, occur when the pictures alone show the action; such pauses are not possible on radio as will be seen in the next transcript.

Although you will get some sense of phonological features from these transcripts, the written form of spontaneous speech used here does not reflect in any great detail the prosodic features of these commentaries; these involve issues such as pace, pitch and loudness. This means that the analysis made here is only a partial reflection of the whole effect.

Activity

Now look closely at a radio version of the same match.

1   What do you notice about the vocabulary used in the radio commentary, particularly where it differs from television?
2   Research some of the ways in which the speech grammar of the radio version differs from that of the television version T1.
3   How does the role of expert summariser on radio differ from that on television?

Radio commentary

C: And David Seaman's got his er spangled colours on again (.) down to our right in the England goal long ball downfield (.) it's time er (.) it's it's difficult to adjust to the colour change here I'm looking at the white shirts and thinking they're English I hope the English players don't have the same problem (.) <u>now Gascoigne</u> finding McManaman for the first time (.) McManaman immediately boxed in by three German defenders (.) brings the ball to the near side to try and find a little room and width (.) still McManaman for England (.) lays the ball to Pearce first cross from Pearce with his left foot headed away by Ziegler only as far as Ince twenty five yards out (.) <u>good effort</u> by Ince turned over fisted over by Kopke corner kick (1)

ES: A tremendous shot by Paul Ince there all a result of Stuart Pearce that familiar loopy cross he has (.) it was cleared at the far post but it came out to Ince (.) and I think he's enjoyed his rest (.) that was a tremendous strike first touch of the game for him (1)

C: He does like to punch the ball does Kopke in that German goal (.) we think he's joining Barcelona Bobby Robson the Barcelona manager is here tonight (.) the former England manager (.) England's first corner of this semi final (.) Gascoigne will take it nearside (.) this is the England left and er (.) referee's not happy (.) with something that's going on on the line (.) little bit of pushing going on there (.) involving McManaman and a German defender Reuter I think (.) here comes the corner teed in by Gascoigne a little header AND SHEARER'S THERE AND ALAN SHEARER SCORES FOR ENGLAND (.) ENGLAND HAVE SCORED (.) AFTER ONLY TWO MINUTES (.) A CORNER KICK FROM GASCOIGNE (.) WAS FLICKED ON AT THE NEAR POST (.) AND ALAN SHEARER CHARGED IN LIKE A BULL AND HEADED THE BALL PAST KOPKE (.) IT'S AN ABSOLUTELY DREAM START FOR THE SEMI FINAL (.) SHEARER HAS GOT HIS FIFTH GOAL OF THE TOURNAMENT (.) WOULD YOU BELIEVE IT (.) IT'S ENGLAND ONE GERMANY NIL (1)

ES: Well tremendous little flick on there by Tony Adams at the near post (.) the ball was weighted in by Gascoigne and just in the six yard box (.) he flicked it on and Alan Shearer running in at pace he doesn't miss from three or four yards the goalkeeper had no chance (.) what a start (1)

C: Incredible (1) Alan Shearer for England (.) they lead by one goal to nil (.) an absolutely fantastic start for the home side here (.) the Germans will now have to come out immediately (.) they can't sit back any more in this game (.) remember in 66 Germany scored first (.) England came from behind to win the game (.) England remember playing the most resilient team in the world (.) the Germans will not lie down but it's an absolutely incredible start for Terry Venables

(473 words)

Commentary

Radio uses many more words than television – this transcript runs to some 473 words – because sound is the only medium of communication; there are no pictures. This absence of pictures is one of the main factors when comparing the radio and television commentaries. The radio version is almost continuous talk – look for instance at the way the following four separate utterances all run into one without a pause: 'good effort by Ince turned over fisted over by Kopke corner kick'. This requirement for almost continuous talk puts the radio commentator under a good deal of pressure and so there are some hesitations and false starts as in; 'it's time er it's it's difficult'. Doubt comes across too, as in 'we think he's joining Barcelona', and 'Reuter I think'. Although the talk is almost continuous, it still makes considerable use of ellipsis. The use of elliptical expression is one of the most obvious ways in which spoken commentary differs from written reports.

A notable feature of the vocabulary of the radio commentary is the use of a whole group of words suggesting disbelief/unreality once the goal is scored; 'an absolutely dream start', 'would you believe it', 'incredible', 'absolutely fantastic', 'absolutely incredible'. Again the absence of pictures is important; the television commentators can hardly deny what viewers have seen with their own eyes, but when only the radio commentator has seen the action, he can give his commentary drama and colour by suggesting he is witnessing something miraculous — an early goal by England. (Note though that in T1 'the bench', not the viewers, are said to be unable to 'quite believe it'.)

Some of the main grammatical features of the television commentary have already been indicated; these include the use of adverbial words and phrases, deictics, the present tense, passive constructions and ellipsis.

The use of adverbials that was noted in the television commentaries is also present in the radio version, but with some additions. The first again involves the fact that there are no pictures, so instead the commentator establishes his viewpoint as the centre of attention, with the match going on around him: 'down to our right in the England goal', 'to the near side', 'nearside'. In the infancy of commentary on the radio, listeners were issued with a plan of the pitch divided into squares. One commentator would comment on the action, while another periodically would call out the number of the square. A pass back to the goalkeeper became 'back to square one', an idiom that has remained in the language long after this form of commentary was abandoned.

Another use of adverbials found in the radio commentary is to do with time. Because there are no pictures to give a sense of continuity of time, the radio commentator needs to fill this gap — he does so when he says, 'now Gascoigne finding McManaman' and 'still McManaman for England'. The absence of pictures also means that adverbial phrases sometimes do the job of the deictics found in the television version: 'here's Ince' becomes 'only as far as Ince'. Throughout the extract only 'there' and 'that' are used, not 'here' and 'this', presumably because no action replays are being shared.

Both television and radio commentaries use mainly, but not exclusively, the present tense, although there is some variation in the use of verbs. Television commentators often use the verb 'to be', especially with deictics as in 'here's Ince', 'that's a good strike', whereas the radio commentator often omits the verb to be, as in '[it is] still McManaman', and in the passive constructions 'McManaman [is] immediately boxed in' and '[is] turned over'.

Other elliptical forms in the radio commentary, all used to help the commentator keep up with the action, include the omission of pronouns '[he] brings the ball', the omission of articles '[a] good effort', 'first cross from Pearce', and the use of a phrase 'the former England manager', instead of a relative clause 'who is the former England manager'.

An important grammatical feature to look at when comparing radio and television commentaries is the different **speech syntax**, which contributes to the overall **cohesion** of what is being said. Writing can be carefully planned and organised, which allows intricate sentence structure, sentences organised into paragraphs and the whole process helped by punctuation and layout. Speaking, though, is not like this; it is spontaneous, unplanned, responding to events as they happen. The commentators on both radio and television are having to think while they talk, and probably listen to instructions from their headphones too. Their talk is also different from casual conversation, though, in that they are not actually speaking to anyone specific − their audience is out there, unseen, and so they receive none of the visual feedback which is so vital in one-to-one conversation.

It is important, then, when looking at the speech syntax of the different commentaries, to remember the following:

1   Speech syntax is different from written syntax, and if we use the term 'speech syntax' we must remember not to see it as an imperfect version of the written model.
2   The speech syntax of sports commentary often differs from that of conversation.
3   The syntax of television sports commentary often differs from that of the radio version.

The fact that speech syntax often differs from written syntax can be seen from the way it appears in the transcripts printed in this unit. Without punctuation and other formal features of organisation it is not always easy to see where a unit of sense begins and ends. Transcripts, for this reason, are often much harder to read than written texts. This does not mean, though, that speech is disorganised, nor that it is unsystematic in its production. After all, the commentaries made perfect sense to audiences at the time.

The point at which England score their goal is a useful point at which to compare the speech syntax of television and radio. In this case transcript 1 will be used as the example of television commentary.

T1 (television)

flick on <u>AND</u> <u>SHEARER</u> (2) <u>WONDERFUL</u> START (1) HIS FIFTH GOAL IN HIS FIFTH MATCH [camera on manager, etc.] THEY CAN'T QUITE BELIEVE IT ON THE BENCH (1) [camera on supporters] in the European championship (.) before coming here it took him twenty three to score five goals (.) when it's mattered <u>most</u> [action replays of goal] (1) Gascoigne's corner (.) flick on by Adams and <u>in</u> by Shearer

Radio

here comes the corner teed in by Gascoigne a <u>little header</u> AND SHEARER'S <u>THERE</u> AND ALAN SHEARER <u>SCORES</u> FOR ENGLAND (.) ENGLAND HAVE <u>SCORED</u> (.) AFTER ONLY TWO MINUTES (.) A CORNER KICK FROM GASCOIGNE (.) WAS FLICKED ON AT THE NEAR POST (.) AND ALAN SHEARER CHARGED IN LIKE A <u>BULL</u> AND HEADED THE BALL PAST KOPKE (.) IT'S AN ABSOLUTELY <u>DREAM</u> START FOR THE SEMI FINAL (.) SHEARER HAS GOT HIS <u>FIFTH</u> GOAL OF THE TOURNAMENT (.) WOULD YOU BELIEVE IT (.) IT'S ENGLAND ONE GERMANY NIL (1)

The pauses in the television commentary act as distinct breaks in the flow of commentary, with the accompanying pictures helping to maintain the overall cohesion. The way pictures affect what is said is shown by the way the utterance 'his fifth goal in his fifth match in the championship' is broken by 'they can't quite believe it on the bench'; the commentator is forced to respond to what he sees on the screen before completing what he intended to say. This balance between language and pictures means that phrases are often used as complete utterances. Noun phrases like 'and Shearer', 'wonderful start' act as complete utterances, making full sense when seen alongside the pictures. The action replay leads to more phrases – the noun phrase 'Gascoigne's corner', the adverbial phrase 'when it mattered most', the noun phrase 'flick on by Adams'. The final phrase 'in by Shearer' omits the verb entirely, the preposition 'in' standing in place of 'it was headed into the goal by Shearer'.

The radio version has no pictures to help cohesion, so the language has to do the complete job. The micro pauses, marked (.), are often short breaths rather than syntactical breaks, and so utterances such as 'Alan Shearer scores for England' and 'England have scored after only two minutes' are much closer to the syntactical units found in writing. 'England have scored after only two minutes', for instance, has a subject ('England') a verb ('have scored') and an adverbial ('after two minutes'). You should notice too that the verb this time is in the past tense, describing something that has happened and is over, whereas the television version, which has far fewer verbs, seems to take place in the permanent present that the action replay allows.

The suggestion that radio commentary requires more complex syntax, can be seen in the utterance

A CORNER KICK FROM GASCOIGNE (.) WAS FLICKED ON AT THE NEAR POST (.) AND ALAN SHEARER CHARGED IN LIKE A BULL AND HEADED THE BALL PAST KOPKE

Here there are three clauses, connected each time by 'and' with no elliptical phrasing at all.

One other feature of this radio commentary is the use of 'remember' as in 'remember in 66 Germany scored first' and 'England remember playing the most resilient team in the world'. The word acts as a warning against over-celebration (presuming that the audience supports England) but is also this commentator's way of informing the audience without appearing to be too all-knowing. He is really telling them things, not reminding them.

The most noticeable difference in the role of the expert summariser is that while the summarisers talk over the action replays, and to some extent what they say is controlled by this, the radio commentator has to give the listeners a verbal replay, giving a second description of the action. At this point in the game the television summarisers provide rather more tactical insight than their radio counterpart. You should remember, however, that these commentaries are unusual in that they record a key piece of action, a goal being scored — for vast stretches of a match the expert will intervene, either during the live action or during a lull in the action. Radio, incidentally, increasingly makes use of action replays, but, unlike television, not during a commentary; it tends to use them in trailers for events or in reviews of past action.

Extension

Comparing different types of sporting text are popular research topics among students. The two units on commentary have introduced some analysis of a highly specialised and in many ways sophisticated form of talk and focused on some of the differences between radio and television football commentary. Further research could involve, among many possibilities:

◎   Analysing and comparing the spoken commentary of other sports, such as athletics, golf, horse racing, tennis, cricket
◎   Comparing the way an event is talked about to how it is written about in newspapers
◎   Analysing how commentary has changed in response to technological developments

Sportswriting I

Writing about sport comes in many forms and serves many purposes. For students who wish to research sportswriting there is a vast amount of material available, so it is important that the focus of the research is clearly located.

1   Make a list of the different types of sportswriting, such as match reports, statistics, etc.
2   For each type that you have listed, try to identify the primary purpose which lies behind the writing – is it to persuade, inform, entertain or instruct?

The purposes which lie behind different written texts are often summarised as being: to *entertain*; to *instruct*; to *persuade*; and to *inform*. These are useful general headings, although in reality texts can rarely be categorised so easily. Newspaper coverage of a sporting event is likely to inform in an entertaining sort of way. A football club fanzine will want to entertain its readers while at the same time putting forward a persuasive point of view. The reference to readers is an important one; not only is it important to explore the purpose of a text but also its likely intended audience. This unit will give examples of the four purposes mentioned above, but will also try to show how more subtle definitions are required if the writing is to be understood fully.

Many comics for younger readers, especially those which flourished after the Second World War, give considerable space to fictional sporting heroes. The main purpose of these comic strip stories is to entertain readers, but they nearly always contain a moral, persuasive, dimension too – heroes (and occasionally heroines) are usually modest and talented, and play very strictly by the rules, therefore acting as role models for young readers. Increasingly adults are catered for by magazines which range from glossy publications devoted to a wide range of specialist sports, to the humbler fanzines, which are largely a product of technological development. The personal computer now allows small groups of fans, with little financial support, to produce their own publications. Fanzines aim to entertain, but they often do so in an irreverent and disrespectful way, challenging accepted views and figures in the games they cover. Fanzines, then, have articles which are also persuasive.

There are numerous examples of instructional publications and manuals about sports, although their shelf life tends to be quite short. New techniques and new ways of looking at the game soon replace the older ones, and the language of instruction changes too. One way of investigating the language of these manuals is to compare a modern version with an older one, if you can find one in a a library. In this way you can trace some of the technical changes that a sport has undergone during its development and at the same time how language reflects changing attitudes and values.

Some sportswriting aims to persuade readers to take a particular point of view. Politicians often write about the benefits of sport to a nation's well-being, in terms of both physical and spiritual health. A famous counter-example of this view was written by George Orwell in the *Tribune* in 1945. Commenting on a football tour to Britain by the Moscow Dynamo club, he argued against the commonly held idea that sport improves international understanding. He said that 'sport is an unfailing cause of ill-will' and that it 'has nothing to do with fair play. It is bound up with hatred, jealousy, boastfulness, disregard of all rules and sadistic pleasure in witnessing violence: in other words it is war minus the shooting.'

The most obvious source of sportswriting is newspapers: virtually all papers, national and local, have sports pages and some regularly print whole sports sections which are almost separate newspapers in their own right. Indeed some countries, notably Italy, have daily national papers devoted entirely to sport. Included within the sports pages are reports of sporting events, profiles of leading figures, analysis of events to come.

Although the main purpose of much newspaper sports coverage is to inform the reader, it is not really so straightforward. Increasingly sports coverage in newspapers involves gossip, intrigue, the personal lives of the stars – in other words a good deal of sports coverage is more concerned with entertainment than information. Newspapers also wage persuasive campaigns, while Fantasy League competitions are big business, offering readers the *entertainment* of choosing their own teams.

Newspaper journalism accounts for the majority of the sports output, but there is a growing market in sports books too; specialist shops exist in major cities, selling only sports-related titles, and publishing a weekly best-seller list. Just as with other branches of book publishing, there are annual awards for sports books. The followers of some sports have often claimed that writing on their sport constitutes a body of 'literature', the implication being that the sport has a social and cultural status higher than others. Two of the most obvious examples in Britain are cricket and golf, while it is often alleged, at least by those who are making claims for their own interests, that football has no literature worthy of note. The fact that cricket and golf are traditionally middle-class games, whereas football is seen as working-class is significant here – literature, some would have us believe, belongs to an elite group and so lies outside popular culture.

This argument, though, is a sterile one – what is and is not literature is a purely subjective matter. What is of interest involves the different **genres** of writing that exist within sports book publishing: fiction; memoirs; biographies; collected journalism. A recent addition to this field has been the so-called 'new sportswriting' in which authors blend accounts of sport with wider perspectives on their lives and experience. A well-known example of this sort of writing is Nick Hornby's *Fever Pitch*. Some examples of writing taken from books will be looked at in the next unit.

Although it is useful to look at the purpose of a piece of sportswriting, you need to guard against over-simple conclusions; often there will be a combination of purposes. Once you have thought about the purposes, you also need to consider the *audience*, for this too will shape the language used.

The two units on writing will look at a sample of some of the many sporting texts available. In addition to purpose and audience, other features will be explored. These are shown in the 'Framework for looking at texts', printed below. This is an edited version of a section from *The Reading Repertoire* published as part of the LINC project (1992). The terms in bold print are useful to remember when analysing texts, and the questions which follow help you to identify more precisely some of the important areas to look at.

Framework for looking at texts

1 **Purpose** What does this text want? What can be deduced about the writer's intentions? Are these intentions openly stated or are they hidden? What kind of reading does this text require?

2 **Audience** Who is being spoken to? What kind of audience is being addressed and how can you tell? Are assumptions being made about the reader of this text?

3 **Narrative** Who 'speaks' the text? Is there an 'I' or 'we' in the text? Does the writer address the reader directly or through an adopted persona? How are the different parts of the text organised?

4 **Genre** What kind of text is this? What other texts does it remind you of? What form does it take? What recognisable conventions has the writer used?

5 **Reader response** What does this text mean to the reader? How is the reader persuaded to interpret it?

6 **Ideology** What values and beliefs does the text state or imply? How are these values and beliefs shaped by what is known about why and how the text was produced?

When looking at these questions, it is helpful to consider some of the following features:

1 **Presentational** choice of lay-out, type-face, illustrations

2 **Organisational** choice of narrative, thematic organisation, sequence of ideas

3 **Grammatical** choice of verb tenses, person, syntax, punctuation, etc.

4 **Lexical** choice of vocabulary, idiom, metaphor

The comic hero

One of the most famous of all fictional sporting characters is Roy of the Rovers, who has appeared in numerous comic strips for over thirty years.

His magnificent footballing feats have led to his name being synonymous with amazing action – 'it's real Roy of the Rovers stuff' is a common saying among people of a certain age, using a character in a children's comic to describe actual events.

Roy Race played for Melchester Rovers, and although apparently ageless, by the time Text: Roy of the Rovers appeared in *Roy of the Rovers Melchester Magic* (1993) he was player-manager of the team. The story so far is that Melchester are playing lowly Branford in a cup game. Branford have just signed Billy Bateman, a strong young player, who has committed a number of sneaky fouls in the first half, as well as scoring the game's only goal so far (notice how alliterative many of the names are in this story). As we join the action it is half time and several Melchester players are keen to exact revenge on Bateman.

Activity

Discuss, in pairs or groups if possible, the following questions:

1   How does the text, in its language and pictures, present an image of a modern football match?
2   What conventions of comic-book writing are used to tell the story of the second half of the game?
3   Although one purpose of this comic strip is to entertain younger readers, it also has an instructional purpose, putting across a moral point of view. What instructional 'message' is given here?

Commentary

The contemporary feel to the images is created partly by the pictures and partly by the use of language. The players' kit looks modern, with a sponsor's name on the shirts — Panini are the makers of football cards for children, so there is in fact a direct piece of advertising here. The players' varied haircuts have been carefully drawn and the referee strikes a typical pose as he brandishes the red card.

To get the full sense of the story the reader has to understand the conventions of this sort of story-telling. In addition to the action being described by the pictures, a sort of running commentary is provided in a number of ways. Rectangular boxes provide an 'external' commentary, giving key pieces of information such as time passing, the score. Random voices in the crowd give more immediate comments about what is

89

happening, and sometimes the players and officials talk directly, signalled by the conventional bubbles connected to the speaker in a continuous line. Some of the most important pieces of language come in the form of thoughts, signalled by the use of bubbles with uneven edges, shaped like clouds, and linked to the thinker's head by a line of smaller bubbles.

Bold print is used to highlight a number of things. Some involve an attempt to indicate features of sound and emphasis used in speech: there is an implied volume of noise in **AAAAGH** and **YESSS**; and a suggested emphasis by the speaker, stressing a point to be made, in '*There'll be **no** retaliation*'. Bold print is also used to highlight a regular feature, something that happens often, as in **Melchester Magic** and **Racey's Rocket**. The narrative, then, is quite a complex one using a series of known conventions to create different 'voices' and effects.

Some of the language of the extract is typical of the specialist terms found in football commentary and reporting: 'cross-ball'; 'professional foul'; 'first-timer'; 'the red card'. Because this is written for a young audience, however, the language is sanitised, and does not contain any of the swearing you would expect to hear from both players and crowd. The nearest we get to any strong language is when the evil Billy Bateman refers to 'those mickey-taking berks', which sounds quaintly old-fashioned.

The story also has a clearly stated ideological viewpoint, putting forward a view of sport which suggests to younger readers that bullies can be defeated by positive values, such as teamwork, skill and a refusal to stoop to the bully's level. In sport, as in life, there are lessons to be learned, but the lessons have to be handed out in the right way. Justice will be done; if the referee misses the cheating, don't worry, the linesman won't. In fact it is the single-handed heroics of Roy, who has himself given the moral teachings, which win the game, but this does not really matter. Notice that it is the moral message, that bullies have to learn the hard way, which has the last word. Lessons to be taught and learned begin and end this extract, pointing clearly to an instructional purpose.

Although this piece of comic-strip writing is aimed at children, the process of analysis that you have gone through can usefully be applied to other texts. Looking at conventions of the genre, at how language is used within the conventions and how the text is underpinned by an ideological viewpoint will help you to analyse other texts. Return now to the Guinness advert in Unit 1 and compare its use of the comic strip with this text.

How to play

Text: Tennis coaching comes from a tennis coaching manual called *The Tennis Workshop* by Alan Jones and Barry Wood. Read the text carefully and then make notes in response to the following questions:

1   How do the organisation and language of this text show that it forms part of a coaching manual?
2   Look in particular at the last two paragraphs, 'Everybody in life ... battle brings'. What features of language can you detect being used here?
3   What ideological values can you detect in the text? Look in particular at what are presented as positive and negative attitudes on the part of the would-be tennis player.

Only in recent years have coaching manuals looked beyond technical skills and contained sections on the more abstract issue of psychological approaches to sport. The title of the section 'The Right Attitude' is positive in its assertion that there is such a thing as a 'right' attitude, and this right attitude is concerned with winning. Although the text is not broken down into a numbered sequence, as it might be if technical skills were being taught, it is nonetheless organised into a series of quite short paragraphs, each one progressing the central argument a stage further, like a skill being developed. These paragraphs often contain brief sentences such as 'Think positively' and 'Remember, most pressure is self-induced'.

One of the most noticeable features of the language is the way that **imperative** verbs are used – the reader is told in no uncertain terms what to do: 'develop the attitude', 'think positively', 'trust yourself', 'do not start to panic', 'believe in yourself'. It is highly likely that instructional writing will give orders, but they are especially noticeable here because the writer is trying to write in a way which emulates the main point – be positive, have no doubt. Usually the reader is addressed either directly or by implication as 'you', but not always; in the second paragraph, for example, 'the player' and 'he' are the points of reference because the reader must not be associated with those who fail. (The authors maintain at the beginning of the book that their use of 'he' includes 'she', but,

91

Text: Tennis coaching

The Right Attitude

Unless it is match point, another point will always come along. Develop the attitude when you play the big point and lose it, that it is just a point. Be the player who can cope with the disappointment of not making the big point. Be the one who has the ability to dismiss it. I have seen many players make an error on a crucial point but then play the next as if it were the beginning of the first set. It is an attitude and skill you have to develop over a period of time.

The player with the less pressure will be quite relaxed, going along merrily and playing quite well. But if he becomes too conscious that he has a lead and senses that he might even win the match, his reaction will be amazing.

To some extent, it is inevitable: we can all play when the pressure does not matter, but the top players have the ability to play under pressure and this is probably one of the most valuable assets you can develop.

Think positively. What is pressure? Where does it come from? Normally it comes from the expectation of winning. Where does this expectation come from? Normally it is based on the past performances of players. A player is expected to win because he has a better chance of winning. If this is pressure, give me more of it!

Remember, most pressure is self-induced.

I am quite certain that most players who have been able to perform at their best have an air of self-possession that says: 'This is the way I play, I'm going to get on with this particular style and if it's not good enough today then that's fair enough.' Overall this attitude definitely works.

If you start to go through a period during which you are not performing to the level you would like, be patient with yourself. Trust yourself. Do not start to panic.

Everybody in life goes through a rough period. Everybody has bad days at the office. Recognise that it will probably be short-lived and get out on the practice court and work as hard as ever. Believe in yourself, and you will come through the crisis. I am quite certain that no matter what style of play the top players are using, this is the philosophy they follow. They may play percentage tennis, or they may go for an all-out attack, but they have the courage to believe in their own style of play.

There will always be mini-crises during the ebb and flow of a match, but nurture the feelings of pleasure and enjoyment the battle brings.

regardless of their intentions, the effect is to suggest an exclusively male narratee.)

The language often expresses certainty. The author (we are not told which of the two authors writes this part) uses a personal 'I' when saying 'I am quite certain that most players ...', the paragraph ending with 'Overall this attitude definitely works'. The narrative, then, is quite a complex one in that sometimes it addresses the reader directly, with 'you' as the focus, sometimes it has the author or 'I' as the focus, and sometimes it is players in general or 'they' who are the focus.

The penultimate paragraph begins with the all-embracing 'everybody' and sets up a contrast between temporary adversity and more permanent triumph. The idea of everybody having 'a bad day at the office' is soon replaced by metaphors of war: 'crisis' and 'mini-crisis' can be overcome by 'all-out attack' and 'courage'. The 'battle' eventually gives 'pleasure and enjoyment'. Again the author is 'quite certain' that what he says is right, provided that you 'believe in yourself'. This time it is top players who are mentioned as being separate from you, the reader; just as you cannot be associated with those who fail, nor are you yet a top player – otherwise why would you need a coaching manual? You, the would-be star, are placed carefully between those who are not to be emulated and those who are.

This extract is concerned solely with the success of the individual. The opponent is never mentioned and winning is the absolute goal of the exercise; pleasure can only be gained through success, and success comes from positive thought centred on self. This positive thought and self-belief must be matched by hard work and an ability to cope with pressure. The author is certain that he is right and he orders you to follow his commands. Ideologically this text belongs very much to a view of sport that is about (male) work and success, rather than one which sees sport as recreation and social interaction.

The fans' view

Football fanzines contain a wide variety of texts written by a large number of usually unpaid, amateur authors. Some texts are designed to entertain an audience which has one certain thing in common with the author, they all support the same team; some texts provide information, such as travel tips on away grounds. Football fanzine authors sometimes have another purpose, though, and that is to write persuasively, to argue a case. Fanzines emerged in the 1980s, a period when British football was in turmoil, rocked by disasters at Bradford and Hillsborough, threatened by hooliganism and racism. The government was keen to legislate on a number of issues, including identity cards. Out of this turmoil came fanzines, which while showing often fanatical support for a team, also argued for greater involvement by fans in the running of football.

Text: Rangers written in the late 1980s, comes from a fanzine called *Follow Follow*, which supports Glasgow Rangers, the leading Scottish team. It was written soon after they had signed a black player, Mark Walters. He was the first black player to play for Rangers.

Text: Rangers

BLUE – THE ONLY COLOUR THAT MATTERS

The creative wing and midfield play of Mark Walters since he signed from Aston Villa has graced every pitch he has played on north of the border.

Unfortunately the fact that he's black has led sizeable sections of morons in other clubs to overlook his skills. His reception at Parkhead and Tynecastle put back their efforts to somehow portray themselves as "progressive" or "family" clubs. In marked contrast Rangers fans have given Mark tremendous support in face of the hostility and sickening racism that he's been subjected to. If a handful of nazis have stopped going to the Stadium then that's great – we're better off without such scum soiling the club.

We don't claim that Rangers fans are angels, if another team had signed a black man then no doubt a minority would have disgraced us by their behaviour – no doubt "inspired", like the Tims and the Jam Tarts, by the juvenile antics of racist clubs in England. Indeed, when we played Chelsea and Ajax a couple of coloured guys came in for abuse – simply due to ignorance and copy-cat behaviour.

Some rabid Tims, like ex-Chelsea player Pat Nevin, displayed their usual paranoia over the Gers and claimed that the abuse "rang around the park", – CRAP. The only place it rang around was in the thick empty heads of the doughballs stupid enough to believe themselves better than another person because of their colour. The vast majority of supporters sat, or stood, embarrassed, silent and angry – helpless to counter the rubbish.

It's good to see that Mark's presence has encouraged many more members of Glasgow's minority communities to come along and support the team. Even before he arrived a poll showed that 80% were Gers fans. They're more than welcome.

When Mark eventually leaves we hope that his stay will have ensured that abuse from the stands and terraces populated by Rangers fans will be directed against players because of their lack of skill and not their colour.

Read the article carefully and make notes on the following questions:

1   How does the language of this text show that the author is writing for a clearly defined audience? What are some of the characteristics of this audience?
2   How does the author develop a persuasive argument in this text, and what is his argument? Look in particular at the language used to describe those the author approves of and those who are disapproved of.

Commentary

The text is full of specialist terms and references which the author assumes the audience will understand; they provide a common language of comradeship and team identity. They do not need explaining for the original audience, indeed cannot be if they are to act as a bonding agent, but it may help readers of this book to know that Parkhead is the home ground of Celtic (the Tims) and that Tynecastle is the home ground of Hearts (the Jam Tarts). Celtic and Hearts were Rangers' leading rivals at the time the article was written, so they form obvious targets for the author to attack. Rangers' ground is simply called the Stadium (its full name is Ibrox Stadium) because the author feels safe in the assumption that the readers know where the ground is.

In one sense the authors of fanzines construct not only a text but a typical reader or narratee as well. It may be that some casual readers of the fanzine would not understand all the references above, but the author has written it to give the impression that one supporter is speaking to fellow, like-minded supporters. The inclusive plural pronoun 'we', used throughout the article, also helps to give this effect. The informality of the language, and the nature of the argument, suggest that the author has in mind a number of features of the typical reader: he is male, white, young, working class. 'Morons', 'nazis . . . scum', 'crap', 'doughballs', are terms of abuse for outsiders, those who support different clubs or who hold racist views. On the other hand the author, who we must assume does not know the player, calls Mark Walters just 'Mark' by the end of the article; Mark is a friend of them all.

The process of persuasion, however, is rather more complex than may first appear. The author's real target is not the easy one of other clubs' supporters, but the racist conduct of some Rangers fans – many of whom will almost certainly be male, white, young and working class. These racist fans will share the author's enthusiasm for the club and so may read the fanzine and this article. The author therefore has to be very careful in framing the argument; other supporters can be abused and alienated, but it would not work to do the same with your own. On the other hand the racists who support Rangers must be persuaded to change their attitudes.

The article begins with a clear statement of Walters' ability – 'he has graced every pitch', which means that any discussion about him must be in the context of his being a good, elegant player. This is followed by attacks on other clubs, the ritual enemy. Whereas these clubs have shown 'hostility and sickening racism', Rangers fans have given 'tremendous support'. So far the article has followed a predictable line, with the opposition criticised, the home fans approved. But the next sentence suggests all is not well at home, there are racist Rangers fans also. The force of the words 'nazis ... scum' is balanced by 'a handful' (in other clubs it is 'sizeable sections'). The author is careful to suggest that racist Rangers supporters are a minority, they are outsiders compared to the vast majority of true supporters. If racists are the real target audience of this article, then they are made to feel outside the the warmth and security of the majority.

We then discover that Rangers have something of a history of racial abuse of players, but again the effect is subtly dissipated by blaming the English for setting the example, and other Scottish clubs for following it. Critics of Rangers, such as Pat Nevin, are roundly abused for making too much of minority behaviour; the majority meanwhile are portrayed as being 'helpless' to do anything about the 'rubbish'.

The penultimate paragraph talks of the positive influence of Walters in attracting new fans, although there is a statistical vagueness about this process, and the final paragraph ends on the 'hope' that abuse in future will be directed only at unskilful footballers. The author, then, is in fact arguing against racism at Rangers – 'blue is the only colour that matters' – but to do so he has employed a number of persuasive strategies to ensure that the readers who agree with him are not offended, and that racists are persuaded to change their behaviour. Racist readers are persuaded to change their behaviour by being urged to join the majority of Rangers fans, and at the same time be opposed to the majority of fans of other clubs.

The moral message, then, is delivered through traditional ideas of group identity, hatred of other groups and a sense of superiority.

Telling it like it is

The final text in this unit is an example of informative journalism, taken from an American local newspaper, the *Belleville News-Democrat*. It consists of a report of a local league baseball game and has been included to give an example of American sports coverage and its use of language.

Text: Baseball

Waterloo blanks Smithton in Legion baseball

By David Wilhelm

Belleville News-Democrat

SMITHTON — Waterloo applied the pressure and never relaxed Saturday as it coasted to a 10-0 victory in five innings over Smithton in an American Legion baseball game.

Waterloo scored a run in the first, two in the second, one in the third and six more in the fourth, giving left-handed pitcher Cody Frederick more than enough support.

Frederick, buoyed by a comfortable lead, used a big breaking curveball to complement his fastball, limiting Smithton to just two singles. Frederick walked three and struck out seven.

"When he gets ahead — like any good pitcher, for that matter, when they get ahead — all they do is throw strikes and let the defense make the plays," Waterloo manager Steve King said. "That's what he did today.

"Cody threw real well. He had very good control of his curveball and he mixed things up. He did a very effective job."

Waterloo, which also was scheduled to play Marissa later Saturday, improved its record to 15-5 overall and 12-3 in the South Division of District 22.

Smithton (6-13 overall) still was alive until Waterloo erupted in the fourth. The big hit was Marty Seitz's wind-blown, three-run double off the left-field wall against losing pitcher.

"It was a tough play," Webb said. "When it's that high and in the sun, with wind, it's pretty tough."

Hitting, however, was Smithton's primary downfall.

"You've got to hit," Webb said. "When your bats are cold, you're cold. We've got potential here, but you've got to hit to get runs. One game we're up, one game we're down. But I can't take anything away from their pitcher. He had good control."

Smithton's only hits were by Dustin Bruggemann and Jason Schlesinger.

Sturgeon surrendered six hits and two walks in four innings before being relieved by Andy Schneider in the fifth. Four of Waterloo's six runs in the sixth were unearned, thanks to an error on Smithton left fielder Jeremy Schmittling.

By then, however, Smithton already trailed 6-0.

"That's the idea, to get on top and do the fundamental things," King said. "That's what we did. Our players are doing the job."

John Rheinecker's sacrifice fly in the first gave Waterloo a 1-0 lead. Shane Yearian's blooper to center in the second bounced off the hard ground and over the head of Smithton center fielder Jason Glaenzer to score Seitz.

"This is a pretty tough diamond as far as (bad) hops and dirt," Webb said. "They've been working on it for quite a while and it's getting better. It's like concrete (in the out-field). When you get the ball that bounces over a 6-foot man's head, it's hard."

The next batter, Jeff Henneberry, drove in Yearian with an RBI grounder to make it 3-0. Drew Dennison's sacrifice fly scored Brad Wacker in the third and increased Waterloo's lead to 4-0.

"We've been hitting the ball pretty well," King said. "We've earned pretty much all our wins. We do the basic fundamentals right. We're playing well, we're executing and we're getting a lot of kids playing time."

Activity

Working with a partner, if possible, discuss the following questions. After this, write your own commentary on the text, using the questions as a framework for your response.

1   This is essentially a piece of informative writing, about a baseball game. How is the information organised in the text? Look in particular at:

◎   The content of each paragraph
◎   The sequence in which the story of the match is told – tracking the scorelines will help you to do this
◎   The part played by quotations

2   The writer of the text has the expectation that readers will understand the language of baseball. Assuming that you are unfamiliar with the game, explore the technical language of baseball, saying which terms you can guess at and which you do not understand at all.

3   What attitudes to sport can be identified through looking at the language used by the two team managers, King and Webb?

Extension

There is a huge amount of sportswriting that you can use for research purposes, some of which has been suggested in this unit. It is important, however, to have a clear sense of purpose, knowing exactly what you want to do, how you want to do it, and the written texts which it will be best to use. A sharp focus is particularly important; general titles such as 'Football Reports in Newspapers' are too general and ill-defined, and so they always lead to an unsatisfactory conclusion.

1   It is much better to look at a specific type of writing, such as instruction manuals and then find some points for investigation. These could be a comparison of two different manuals produced for different audiences, or you could compare a modern manual with an older one.

2   If you can find some old comics, it would be interesting to compare sport comic strips of an earlier age with those of the present day.

3   Because the language of speaking and writing are so different, you could use some of the ideas in Units 5 and 6 and investigate the difference between spoken and written accounts of the same sporting event.

Sportswriting II

In the previous unit on writing, the examples came from texts such as comics, manuals, fanzines and newspapers, texts with a fairly brief shelf life. In this second unit on writing the texts will come from books on sport, works which are more substantial, in that they are longer and more sustained in what they have to say. The three books referred to here were all published in the 1990s and approached sport in an interesting, often personal way. Looking at the language used by the three authors will show how some contemporary writers view sport as part of a larger social picture.

Nick Hornby's book *Fever Pitch*, first published in 1992 is described on its front cover as 'the best football book ever written', whereas on the back cover it is described as 'a sophisticated study of human obsession, families, masculinity, class, identity, growing up, loyalty, depression and joy'. Reviewers often like to place a text, to ascribe it to a certain genre, so clearly this book meant very different things to different reviewers. To one it was simply a book about football, to the other a study of wide-ranging sociological and philosophical issues. Its title, *Fever Pitch*, hints at both these readings; on the one hand it alludes to the football pitch the game is played on, on the other it suggests the state of mind of the obsessive football fan.

Starting with the first Arsenal football match Hornby saw in 1968, *Fever Pitch* consists of a series of chapters, each with a title and each labelled also with a football match and a date. In a chapter called 'The

I did learn, in the end. I learned that my threatening anybody was preposterous – I might just as well have promised the Coventry fans to bear their children – and that in any case violence and its attendant culture is uncool (none of the women I have ever wanted to sleep with would have been particularly impressed with me that afternoon). The big lesson, though, the one that tells you football is only a game and that if your team loses there's no need to go berserk ... I like to think I've learned that one. But I can still feel it in me, sometimes, at away games when we're surrounded by opposing fans and the referee's giving us nothing and we're hanging on and hanging on and then Adams slips and their centre-forward's in and then there's this terrible needling bellow from all around you ... Then I'm back to remembering just two of the three lessons, which is enough in some ways but not enough in others.

Masculinity has somehow acquired a more specific, less abstract meaning than femininity. Many people seem to regard femininity as a quality; but according to a large number of both men and women, masculinity is a shared set of assumptions and values that men can either accept or reject. You like football? Then you also like soul music, beer, thumping people, grabbing ladies' breasts, and money. You're a rugby or a cricket man? You like Dire Straits or Mozart, wine, pinching ladies' bottoms and money. You don't fit into either camp? *Macho, nein danke?* In which case it must follow that you're a pacifist vegetarian, studiously oblivious to the charms of Michelle Pfeiffer, who thinks that only leering wideboys listen to Luther Vandross.

It's easy to forget that we can pick and choose. Theoretically it is possible to like football, soul music and beer, for example, but to abhor breast-grabbing and bottom pinching (or, one has to concede, vice versa); one can admire Muriel Spark *and* Bryan Robson. Interestingly it is men who seem to be more aware than women of the opportunities for mix 'n' match: a feminist colleague of mine literally refused to believe that I watched Arsenal, a disbelief that apparently had its roots in the fact that we had once had a conversation about a feminist novel. How could I possibly have read the book *and* have been to Highbury? Tell a thinking woman that you like football and you're in for a pretty sobering glimpse of the female conception of the male.

And yet I have to accept that my spiteful fury during the Coventry game was the logical conclusion to what had begun four years before. At fifteen I was not capable of picking and choosing, nor of recognising that this culture was not necessarily discrete. If I wanted to spend Saturdays at Highbury watching football, then I also had to wave a spear with as much venom as I could muster. If, as seems probable given my sporadically fatherless state, part of my obsession with Arsenal was that it gave me a quick way to fill a previously empty trolley in the Masculinity Supermarket, then it is perhaps understandable if I didn't sort out until later on what was rubbish and what was worth keeping. I just threw in everything I saw, and stupid, blind, violent rage was certainly in my field of vision.

I was lucky (and it *was* luck, I can take no credit for it) that I nauseated myself pretty quickly; lucky most of all that the women I fancied, and the men I wanted to befriend (at this stage those verbs belonged exactly where I have placed them), would have had nothing to do with me if I hadn't. If I'd met the kind of girl who accepted or even encouraged masculine belligerence then I might not have had to bother. (What was that anti-Vietnam slogan? 'Women say yes to men who say no'?) But there are football fans, thousands of them, who have neither the need nor the desire to get a perspective on their own aggression. I worry for them and I despise them and I'm frightened of them; and some of them, grown men in their mid-thirties with kids, are too old now to go around threatening to kick heads, but they do anyway.

Whole Package: Arsenal v Coventry 4.11.72' Hornby describes the first time he joined in abusive chants against the opposition supporters when he was aged 15. Now, as the adult writing the book, he feels embarrassment at his behaviour, and as Text: Fever Pitch begins he talks about lessons that he has learned from the experience.

Activity

Discuss, in groups if possible, the following questions and make notes on your findings to share with others.

1   To what extent is this an account of a football match in the traditional sense of reporting a game?
2   What would you say is the main topic being covered in each of the five paragraphs? When you look at how the paragraphs are organised, what do you discover about the text as a whole?
3   What issues, from the list given in the second review above, are mentioned in this extract? What is said about these issues? Can you detect any points of view being put across?

Commentary

This is clearly not an account of a football match as you might find it in a newspaper. Although the opposition − Coventry − are mentioned a couple of times, it really could be any match that is being talked about. No final score is given, there is no description of any action on the pitch. The repeated use of the first person pronoun 'I' (29 times in this extract) clearly places the narrator at the centre of the text, rather than any sporting action. It is his own behaviour that he is interested in, not the players', although he expands beyond his own experience to look more generally at the behaviour of men. Reflecting as an adult on his teenage self, he seeks to explain why he threatened violence and whether he is still capable of it.

The organisation of the paragraphs, the narrative structure of the extract, reveals a great deal about the text:

Paragraph 1 personal lessons learned by the narrator – and occasionally forgotten
Paragraph 2 the apparent meaning of 'masculinity' and how it encompasses a shared set of assumptions
Paragraph 3 the possibility of individual choice for men – and the assumptions women make about them
Paragraph 4 the narrator returns to his past and a reference to family problems
Paragraph 5 his own rejection of violence compared to many men who continue to be violent – a synthesis of the personal and the general

---

Note: The term narrator is used here to desribe the 'voice' which is 'speaking' the text. Although it is tempting to suggest that in a text which is so obviously autobiographical it must be the author who is speaking the text, this is not necessarily so. The very process of writing, of constructing and shaping the text, means that the narrative voice too has been constructed.

What this outline of the paragraphs shows is that the text is a mixture of personal anecdote and wider cultural analysis, which means that the serious issues such as masculinity, male behaviour, families are looked at very much from a personal perspective, without any great detail or academic rigour. The discussion of male behaviour is based on 'somehow' and 'seem' rather than any scientific evidence; only one 'feminist colleague' is enough for him to build a theory on. The cultural origins of the 'Masculinity Supermarket' are not explored.

In his last paragraph, where he places his own experience alongside continuing violence among football fans, we may expect a set of answers, of clear opinions, but because the writing is centred on personal experience we get something much more tentative. The use of brackets suggests a point of view that is uncertain and it is the narrator's 'I' that returns to centre stage. The verbs are about feelings rather than rationally deduced arguments: 'worry', 'despise', 'I'm frightened'. The paragraph ends on an uncertain note, on the anti-climax of the word 'anyway'.

This may mean that some readers will feel that the analysis of important issues does not go far enough, while others will want to know more about the reference to 'sporadic fatherlessness' which hints at a more autobiographical approach. The text cannot be easily placed into a genre; it is about sport, about an individual's experience, about cultural issues which are accessible partly because they are not rigorously developed. All these features combine to give the sense of a 'new' form of sportswriting which contributed to the book's popularity. If this short extract is taken as typical of the whole book, then *Fever Pitch* is neither a book of sports reportage nor an academic work on sociological issues – and there are plenty of books which are in both of these categories. Instead, sport is used as a starting point for both personal reflection and for the discussion of a range of social issues – so once again sport is seen as part of our social fabric rather than something lying outside it.

Donald McRae's *Dark Trade* is subtitled *Lost in Boxing* and was published in 1996, the year in which it won the award for Sports Book of the Year. Both title and sub-title are worth investigating more closely. Boxing as a sport has had a consistently bad press for a number of years. It is riddled with factions, it is corrupted by large sums of money, it has recently suffered from a spate of fatal or near-fatal injuries. It is dark in the sense that it is corrupt, a trade because its main interest is in the making of money. The fact that most boxers in Britain and America are black gives another association to the title; the dark trade, like the slave trade, exploits its victims using their labours to enrich others. The sub-title *Lost in Boxing* carries an ambivalence of meaning too – who is lost in boxing, the fighters or the audience? And in what sense lost? Lost in the sense of 'defeated' or lost in the sense of 'captivated by'?

McRae's title and sub-title give a number of clues as to the nature of the book. It would be impossible for an intelligent writer to view boxing uncritically, and McRae does indeed shed light on many of the dubious practices of the sport. At the same time, though, he is himself captivated by the sport, at times lost in it, to the extent that he wants to explore even its darkest moments, when fighters suffer awful injuries. The sport itself cannot withstand close scrutiny, but there are moments when it can produce action which its followers find compelling. As with *Fever Pitch*, *Dark Trade* uses sport as a starting point, this time for an analysis of people's reaction to the legitimised violence of boxing.

Text: Dark Trade

WATSON came in for the kill. It was then that he was hit. The punch landed in a scything arc which pundits would have termed "perfect" if it had not wrought such havoc. The impact on Michael Watson's jaw knocked him off his feet. He landed on his back. He was down and all but out. None of us saw it then but Michael Watson's head rocked hard against the third and lowest rope. For a hundredth of a second his head may have rested there, as if cribbed in a cat's cradle made out of an elastic band by a child. But then it snapped back, the rope inducing more of a whiplash than Eubank's right hand. Watson struggled up, looking more groggy than Eubank had done only an instant before. The bell rang — for the end of that round and, as we now know, something far worse.

Jimmy Tibbs and his corner were devastated. They showered water over their stricken fighter, buffing him around the face tenderly, asking "are you okay ... are you all right?" I saw Michael Watson nod. But from where I sat it was impossible to see into his eyes. He staggered up on spindly legs for the final round.

It was the one moment we had all been waiting for, that cataclysmic finale, a blinding finish where one fighter "takes out" the other, where a man lurches against the ropes and tries to stop himself being swallowed up in blackness, where one boxer wins and the other loses, where all our innate ferocity and misery gets buried with those punches and we supposedly come out of his knockout feeling exhilarated and drained of shabby desire. I wanted to see if Watson could survive the inevitable assault, if he could somehow drag himself from the hole into which he'd fallen. Neither I nor anyone else around me wanted our climax, that certain knockout, to be denied. The grace and skill of Watson in the preceding rounds were forgotten. He was slipping away and yet we still wanted to see a few more punches — as much from him as Eubank.

Eubank rushed towards him with flailing arms. Most of his shattered punches missed. After 20 seconds, with Watson creaking like a badly hacked tree, Roy Francis stepped between the fighters. They disappeared from view as the ring was engulfed. Hundreds of people clambered towards the ropes as if by coming close enough they could convince themselves of the truth.

The next few minutes are lost forever. I was only returned to reality by the sight of Eubank's face on a television monitor a few feet away. I watched him talking but could only hear the scuffle which had broken out on the edge of the ring between two rival groups of fans. Eubank hollered at Gary Newbon, the ITV interviewer, "I want him tested. I want him tested to see if he has anything in his blood. Because he was too ... he was so strong. I want his urine tested because no one can be that strong ... "

I turned away — feeling sick with the frenzy of the night — and walked up the same aisle which Michael Watson had marched down only an hour before with the crowd singing his name.

Like one of those gaping pedestrians at a roadside accident I succumbed to the horror of the crash. I wanted to look away but I couldn't, I wanted to leave but I didn't. Through the lemony haze of the floodlights I knew that that eleventh-round punch from Eubank had been what I always wanted to see most in a ring. The kind of last-gasp blow which turns defeat into stunning victory. It was a punch, a lethal uppercut, which yanked me from my seat and left me senseless of everything but the sheer spectacle of men working feverishly on each fighter as they slumped down on their tiny stools.

When else as an adult, if not in sex or sleep, had I been so beyond the mundane? There was a difference when Arsenal scored a last-minute winner, or when I disappeared into the closing page of a book or the last scene of a film. Those moments were all imitations of life — whereas that single blow had distilled life so graphically that it conjured up images of death.

But I'd wanted to see that punch; to say that I had witnessed the most unexpected reversal in the ring. I also wanted the conclusive triumph of one man over another.

So much of my own life stumbled between two different poles — one marking out a mazed past, the other peering into an unseen future — that I seldom lived wholly in the "now". I had felt more alive, at least in the sense of being aware of nothing but the present, in those few minutes spanning the eleventh and twelfth.

But after it was waved to an end I needed the extraordinary to be subsumed by the ordinary again. I wanted both boxers to get up, to hug and even kiss each other, to say "what a fight, man, what a fight — but it's over now ..."

But, still, we waited for Watson to get up.

The extract in Text: Dark Trade (slightly abridged) forms the closing paragraphs of a chapter from Donald McRae's book on boxing *Dark Trade* (1996). In this chapter he describes being present at a fight in 1991 between Chris Eubank and Michael Watson. Watson, it was believed, was winning the fight until near the end of the penultimate round when Eubank hit him with a punch which caused serious brain damage. This fight, along with a number of others in which boxers either died or suffered serious injury, led to calls for boxing to be banned.

Read the extract carefully at least twice and then, if possible in groups or pairs, discuss answers to the following questions:

1   This is an account written in a book published a number of years after the fight. How does it differ in its language from a newspaper report which would be published immediately after the fight?
2   The jacket for *Dark Trade* describes the book as a 'vivid and illuminating personal journey'. Identify the metaphorical language used by McRae to describe the fight itself and his reactions to it. How does this metaphorical language help to show the author's personal response to what he has seen?
3   Look closely at the last five paragraphs of the extract. Identify some of the main linguistic methods used by McRae in summarising both the fight and his response to it.

Commentary

A piece of journalistic reporting, written and published immediately after the fight, would have focused on the two boxers and their actions, looking at the sequence of events which led to the final result. Here, though, after an opening two sentences which indeed resemble a report of the fight, the focus of attention is as much on the writer and the rest of the crowd as it is on the two boxers. The final minutes of the fight are described, but not in consecutive sentences and paragraphs. As key incidents happen, McRae breaks off to explore his response to them.

The opening words of the second paragraph 'None of us saw it then' indicate that this is a description framed and informed by passing time – the writer has had time to consider and what was not known then is known now ('as we now know'). The use of the **past tense**, as in 'It was the one moment we *had* all been waiting for', also gives a sense of time having passed. This sense of the fight being some time ago, something to reflect on, is balanced by the urgency and immediacy of some of the description. This can be seen in the paragraph beginning 'It was the one moment we had all been waiting for'; this sentence continues with a series of **clauses**, many beginning with the repeated 'where', and is followed by a sentence with clauses beginning with 'if'. The fight is viewed through two time perspectives, one close and immediate, the other more distant, allowing thought and reflection.

Identifying the **pronouns** used in the narrative also helps to distinguish this piece of writing from a straightforward report. 'Us'/'we' appear when the narrator is part of the crowd and its response, but most frequently the narrative pronoun is 'I'. The repeated 'I' means that although the boxing match is the event being described, it is the narrator's personal response, and his own actions, which he is most interested in as he looks back. 'I wanted', 'I watched', 'I knew', 'I needed' place his perceptions and his needs as the central issues under review.

There is a large amount of **metaphorical** language in this extract, much of it referring to the narrator's emotions. His desire is 'shabby' and his interest in the fight is compared to that of 'a gaping pedestrian in a roadside accident'. This metaphorical language suggests that McRae is aware that his fascination with the fight is, in retrospect, something which needs explaining. Watson is left paralysed and yet McRae has watched and been emotionally involved in the fight. Where metaphorical language is used to describe the fight itself, as in the description of Watson's head 'cribbed in a cat's cradle', there is again a sense of the narrator looking back, reflecting on the event – probably literally through watching recordings of the action.

One metaphor, though, which combines events in the ring with the narrator's own responses, comes when he says: 'It was a punch, a lethal uppercut which yanked me from my seat and left me senseless'. The punch which damages Watson so badly does the same, briefly, to the watching narrator. The uncertainty he feels about being there, about watching, is temporarily knocked out of him – he loses his senses, and with them his doubt about the very existence of boxing as a sport. For a moment he feels the full impact of the event, and so is a part of something which his more rational self questions.

In the final paragraphs McRae explores the significance of what he has been watching and what it means to him. This exploration is expressed through balancing opposites – 'life'/'death', 'ordinary'/'extraordinary' – and through repetition of key words – 'I'd wanted'/'I also wanted'/'I wanted'. The antithesis of life and death is especially important here. Many other experiences, sporting or literary, were 'imitations' of life, but this one blow 'distilled' life to the point where it 'conjured up images of death'. Watching this blow gave a life which usually 'stumbled' an experience so sharp that it was 'wholly in the now'. The language carries connotations of a religious experience, of a transfiguring moment.

Another word which is repeated, at the beginning of three paragraphs, is the word 'but'. Although the repetition gives a cumulative effect, the word is used with a slightly different meaning each time: 'But I'd wanted to see that punch' means 'except'; 'But after it was waved to an end' means 'however'; 'But, still, we waited' means 'nonetheless'. The last 'but' breaks the spell of heightened experience and returns narrator, and so reader, back to an awful reality. What is left is Watson seriously injured, motionless. The word 'still' can also be seen to carry several meanings. Although its obvious meaning is to do with time, both McRae and Watson are also, in their different ways, still. And so is the reader, left to picture the horror of the fighter who cannot get up.

Writing documentary

A popular method for writers who want to write a documentary about a sport, or its players, is to spend a season with a team. Pete Davies spent a season with the Doncaster Belles Women's Football Team, looking not only at the most successful team in English women's football, but more broadly at the way the women's game is treated by a male-dominated football hierarchy. Helped in part by Pete Davies's book, women's football has recently gained more publicity, although it still has some way to go to reach the interest shown in 1920, when 53,000 spectators watched a game between two Lancashire sides. This was more than watched the men's FA Cup Final of that year, and within a year the Football Association had banned women from playing on Football League grounds, a ban which remained in force for over fifty years.

The following three short extracts are taken from *I Lost My Heart To The Belles* by Pete Davies. All three extracts come from a chapter called 'Overdose Time'.

Activity

Research answers to the following questions:

1   What features of Davies's writing identify the book as a documentary? Look, for instance, at his use of attributed speech and of factual information.

107

The Belles hated Arsenal. They were only founded in 1987, they were upstarts, big city bigheads, and they were just *Arsenal*, unsmiling, ruthless, professional, fun-free like no other women's team. In '92–'93 they beat the Belles 2–1 before 17,000 at Highbury during a benefit for the boxer Michael Watson, and the result gave them the league. So after the game, said Joanne, 'Us Belles were all singing, messing around – we were disappointed, obviously, but it's a game, we'll have another chance – and them, they were just stood there. If that had been us we'd have been out partying, we always stay together when we've won something – but them, they went home.'

But there's more to it, of course, than just Arsenal being Arsenal, five across the back, only scoring at set pieces. The Belles hated Arsenal because, in '92–'93, in that second season of the women's national league, Arsenal won everything – championship, League Cup, FA Cup too. So then, said Joanne, 'They were going round saying they were tops now, that Belles were past it, when we'd been up there ten years – and you don't suddenly become top team in one season. So we showed them, didn't we? We won it all back.'

— —

It made up for losing – and besides, do the Belles *really* hate Arsenal? No, not really. Hating Arsenal's somewhere between a philosophical dictum and a natural-born thing, and at Arsenal they must have got used to it a million years ago. Besides, women's football's too small and too friendly for hate. At that conceptual level, that level of Platonic footballing essences, you can say you 'hate Arsenal' – but then you see the individuals get together and you know they don't mean it, you know it's only words. You see Kaz and Gail have a chat and a laugh with Marieanne Spacey before the game, international partners; you see Kaz waiting on a goal kick to come her way, leaning a casual arm on Gill Wylie's big shoulder beside her, the two of them smiling – and you know they both know that if they kick each other somewhere down the line it's only in the cause, it's only in the game. Or there's the Belle and the Arsenal girl who dived out behind the clubhouse after the game to share a spliff together, 'cause what the hell – they don't get paid for this, and what's to hate?

In women's football they train, they work, they run their legs off, and they enjoy themselves, win or lose – because otherwise, what on earth would be the point?

— —

And that, of course, is why I drove on down the road after all. Money and TV might be turning the men's game into soap (with astonishing amounts of lather) but in the women's game you still get real people, playing the real game and nothing more. You don't have to take out a second mortgage to watch it, you don't have to buy any merchandise, you don't have to listen to Jimmy Hill at half-time, you don't have to worry whether anybody's bent, and you don't have to watch criminal idiots chucking the furniture on to the heads of small children. It is instead romantic, it's attractive, it's a laugh, it's got its head on its shoulders instead of its snout in a brown envelope, and if your lot lose you're not obliged to believe that the world's come to an end – which, given the state the Belles were in, was probably a very good thing.

2   Davies begins the first extract by saying 'The Belles hated Arsenal',
     but this view gradually alters as you read further. How does Davies
     introduce a more detailed view, and what is he saying about
     women's football in the process?
3   In the final paragraph, Davies argues passionately in favour of
     women's football. How does his language convey this passion? Look
     at grammatical structures as well as vocabulary.

Extension

Many sports books are published each year. They provide plenty of useful
material for project work, but should be approached with some caution.
Many students find it difficult to produce a project based on one book;
you need quite sophisticated skills in the analysis of stylistics if you are to
succeed and you certainly need a very focused title. It is often better to
compare texts, or parts of texts, either across genres (a player's tour
diary compared to a journalist's reports) or across sports (a cricketer's
tour diary compared to a rugby player's).

109

index of terms

This is a form of combined glossary and index. Listed below are some of the key terms used in the book, together with brief definitions for purposes of reference. The page references will normally take you to the first use of the term in the book, where it will be shown in bold.

acronym 47

A word composed of the initial letters of other words and pronounced as a whole word, i.e. FIFA (Federation of International Football Associations) (see also **initialism**).

adverbials 75

Used to describe words, clauses, or phrases which act as adverbs. This means that they add detail and specificity to a verb, often in terms of how, where or when, i.e. 'they played *well*', 'they played *on an old rubbish tip*', 'they played *yesterday*'.

advertorial 13

Used in publishing to describe a piece of text which is part advert, part editorial material. A competition, devised and written by magazine staff, but giving away prizes offered by one particular firm is one possible example.

alliteration 21

A series of words beginning with the same sound. For example 'Billy Bareman of Branford'.

blend word 42

A word formed by the mixing together of parts of two or more other words. A 'fanzine' is a magazine written by fans.

clause 104

A structural unit which is part of a sentence, either as a main clause, which can stand alone and be equivalent to a sentence, or as a subordinate or dependent clause.

code 47

A language variety in which grammar and/or vocabulary are particular to a specific group.

cohesion 79

A term which refers to the patterns of language created within a text, mainly within and across sentence boundaries, and which collectively make up the organisation of larger units of text. Cohesion can be both lexical and grammatical. Lexical cohesion can be established by chains of words of related meaning which link across sentences (see also **semantic field**). Grammatical cohesion is established in a number of ways, including reference terms such as 'the', 'this', 'it', and so on (see **deictics**).

connective 67

A word which links linguistic units such as clauses. Words

such as 'and', but' and 'therefore' are connectives. Another term for connective is conjunction.

connotation 2

The connotations of a word are the associations it creates. A list of connotations of the game of cricket are seen in Unit 1.

deictics 75

Words which point backwards, forwards or outside a text and which situate a speaker or writer in relation to what is said. For example, when a commentator says, 'And this is Damon Hill and that's a superb piece of driving', the deictic words are 'this' and 'that'.

denotation 2

The literal, dictionary definition of a word.

ellipsis 10

The omission of part of a structure. It is normally used for reasons of economy and in spoken discourse can create a sense of informality. It is especially common in sports commentary, where events have to be described as they happen. For example, in the commentary 'Shearer for post' the words 'is standing by the' have been omitted.

filler 67

Items which do not carry conventional meaning, but are used, most frequently in spoken discourse, to allow time to think, to create a pause, and so on. 'Um', 'er' are typical examples.

genre 85, 86

An identifiable text type. It can be used in a number of ways: to identify a type of writing, as in a report, a letter, a poem; and it can identify a group of texts which have subject matter in common, as in detective writing, travel writing, sports writing.

ideology 24, 86

The set of cultural values which lie behind a text or texts. All texts have ideologies: there is no such thing as a 'neutral' text.

imperative 91

The expression of a command.

initialism 47

Phrases that are referred to by their initial letters, i.e. WBO (World Boxing Organisation).

intertextuality 15

The way in which one text echoes or refers to another text or texts. The Guinness advert in Unit 1 uses the conventions and ideas of Roy of the Rovers comic books, for example.

inversion 75

Changing the usual order of items. Inversion is especially common in commentary as in 'at full stretch are the Newcastle defence'.

jargon 48

The technical language of a certain occupation or field of activity. Because the word has increasingly been used critically, to suggest that such language use is deliberately obscure, linguists are cautious about using the term. For a fuller discussion, see Unit 4.

lower case 11

Referring to letters that are 'small' rather than capitals. The words defined in this glossary have been written in lower case, including their first letters.

metaphor   3, 104

A word or a phrase which establishes a comparison or analogy between one object or idea and another. 'The game exploded into life' compares a game with a bomb, for instance.

modifier   40

A word or phrase which adds more detail (or modifies) another element. In the phrase 'the tactically naive captain', the phrase 'tactically naive' acts as a modifier.

name tag   21

A label attached to a name. The football manager Ron Atkinson is often referred to in the press as 'Big Ron'.

narratee   (see **narrator**)

narrator   10

The voice which 'speaks' a text. Where this is obviously an invented voice, the speaker is sometimes referred to as the narrative persona. Just as the narrator can be a constructed voice, so the reader can be a constructed figure too. Narratee refers to a constructed reader for whom the text is supposedly written. There can be more than one narrator and more than one narratee or group of narratees.

noun phrase   10

A group of words which describe a noun. 'The best team in England' is a noun phrase, with the core noun 'team' pre-modified by the words 'the best' and post-modified by the words 'in England'.

passive   (see **voice**)

phatic   67

A term used to describe language, usually in spoken discourse, which establishes and/or maintains social contact, rather than having any precise meaning. For example 'How are you?' does not literally call upon someone to reply with their full medical history.

pronouns   67, 104

Words which normally substitute for nouns or noun phrases 'I', 'you'. For example 'it', 'they', 'their', 'some', 'any', 'this', 'myself'.

pun   15

A comic effect produced by playing with the different meanings of a word, or by suggesting two words which sound the same but have different meanings.

rhetoric   6

Used to refer to persuasive writing or speaking.

semantic field   8

A group of words which are related in meaning as a result of being connected with a particular context of use. 'Shot', 'header', 'tackle', 'throw-in' are all connected with the semantic field of football.

semantics   2

The study of linguistic meaning.

speech syntax   79

Syntax refers to the organisation of sentence structure. The phrase 'speech syntax' has been used in this book when referring to speech events, because the structure of spoken discourse is often very different from that of written discourse.

113

synecdoche 52

The use of part of something to refer to the whole. This is a popular usage in sport; 'the yellow jersey' in cycling is used to refer to the race leader, for instance, and 'the net' in football is used instead of the goal.

tense 104

Mainly associated with a verb in a sentence, marking the time of an action. The two primary tenses in English are the present tense – 'and Gascoigne shoots'; and the past – 'Gascoigne shot wide'.

further reading

Unit 1

Hartley, L.P. (1953) *The Go-Between* (Hamish Hamilton, London).
Macdonell, A.G. (1933) *England Their England* (Macmillan, London).
Marqusee, M. (1994) *Anyone But England* (Verso, London).
Sassoon, S. (1937) *Memoirs of a Foxhunting Man* (Faber & Faber, London).

Unit 2

Davies, P. (1996) *I Lost My Heart To The Belles* (Heinemann, London).

Unit 3

O'Donnell, H. (1994) 'Mapping the mythical: a geopolitics of national sporting stereotypes', in *Discourse and Society*, 5: 3.

Unit 4

Bryson, B. (1994) *Made in America* (Secker & Warburg, London).
Lakoff, G. and Johnson, M. (1980) *Metaphors We Live By* (Chicago University Press, Chicago).

Unit 7

Orwell, G. (1945) 'The sporting spirit', reprinted in *Collected Essays, Journalism and Letters of George Orwell*, Vol. 4 (1970) (Penguin, London).

Unit 8

Hornby, N. (1992) *Fever Pitch* (Gollancz, London).
McRae, D. (1996) *Dark Trade* (Mainstream, Edinburgh).

references

Bryson, B. (1994) *Made in America* (Secker & Warburg, London).

Crystal, D. (1995) *The Cambridge Encyclopedia of the English Language* (Cambridge University Press, Cambridge).

Goddard, A. (1996) *Tall Stories: The Metaphorical Nature of Everyday Talk,* Sheffield, NATE English in Education, vol. 30.

Lakoff, G. and Johnson, M. (1980) *Metaphors We Live By* (Chicago University Press, Chicago).

LINC Materials for Professional Development (1992) (Hodder & Stoughton, London).

Tannen, D. (1991) *You Just Don't Understand: Men and Women in Conversation* (Virago, London).